Ways of Telling

The Work of John Berger

Pluto Press

First published in 1986 by Pluto Press Limited,
The Works, 105a Torriano Avenue, London NW5 2RX
and Pluto Press Australia Limited, PO Box 199, Leichhardt,
New South Wales 2040, Australia. Also Pluto Press,
51 Washington Street, Dover, New Hampshire 03820 USA

7 6 5 4 3 2 1

90 89 88 87 86

The author and publishers are grateful to the following for permission to reprint copyright material: Writers and Readers Publishing Co-operative and Chatto/ Tigerstripe for material from John Berger's writings; Collins Harvill for the poem 'Balzac' from *Fires* by Raymond Carver; Faber & Faber for extracts from the poems 'Dehorning' and 'Bringing in New Couples' from *Moortown* by Ted Hughes; and Pluto Press for the interview with John Berger from *Art, Politics, Cinema*.

Set by Rapidset & Design Ltd., London WC1
Printed in Great Britain by Cox Wyman, Reading, Berks.

British Library Cataloguing in Publication Data
Dyer, Geoff
   Ways of telling: the work of John Berger.
   1. Berger, John—Criticism and
   interpretation
   I. Title
   828'.91408   PR6052.E564Z/

ISBN 0 7453 0097 9

Contents

For Bob Beale and Chris Beal

Acknowledgements

I am indebted to Vron Ware and Nick Kimberley for first giving me the opportunity to write about books, and subsequently to Malcom Imrie and Gillian Wilce; to Pete Ayrton; to Paul Bonnaventura for obtaining some articles for me and putting me in touch with Nick Rowlings who gave me advice at an early stage; to Simon Bradford for letting me see the *Ways of Seeing* programmes; and to Anthony Barnett for reading the manuscript and making many helpful suggestions. More general thanks to all my friends in and around Brixton, especially to Charlie, John, and most of all, to Sue.

My biggest debt, appropriately, is to John Berger himself who has co-operated with and supported this book right from the beginning, without asking to see what I was writing.

Abbreviations

In the text and in the notes and references, the titles of Berger's works are abbreviated as follows:

A.L.	*About Looking*
A.O.F.	*And Our Faces, My Heart, Brief as Photos*
A.R.	*Art and Revolution*
C.F.	*Corker's Freedom*
A.W.O.T.	*Another Way of Telling*
F.C.	*The Foot of Clive*
F.M.	*A Fortunate Man*
L.T.	*Selected Essays and Articles: The Look of Things*
M.C.	*The Moment of Cubism*
P.E.	*Pig Earth*
P.R.	*Permanent Red*
P.T.	*A Painter of our Time*
S.F.P.	*The Success and Failure of Picasso*
S.M.	*A Seventh Man*
W.B.	*The White Bird*
W.S.	*Ways of Seeing*

(For editions, see bibliography.)

Preface

This book is intended for those who – like me when I began working on it – want to know more about John Berger's work. To that extent it is a straightforward piece of exposition and criticism.

While Berger is widely read, and though *Ways of Seeing* has been massively influential, his stature as writer and intellectual has not been adequately recognized. A map of literary reputations (though the word 'literary' is itself too narrow to apply to someone with Berger's range of output) does not properly represent writers' actual achievements. Ultimately the hope of this book is not that Berger's name may figure more prominently on that map but that his *example* will enable us fundamentally to alter its shape; that he may be seen not as an exception but as a model. More realistically, this book can only attempt a more modest intervention. I would have it seen not as the work of an academic critic but as an extended response from an interested and grateful reader, as a prolonged attempt to encourage others to experience something that I have particularly enjoyed.

I should also draw the reader's attention to two conspicuous absences: first, there is a minimum of biographical information; for the purpose of this study we assume, in Gauguin's phrase, that 'the work of a man is the explanation of that man'. Second, I do not discuss the films he wrote with Alain Tanner: *The Salamander* (1971), *The Middle of the World* (1974), *Jonah Who Will Be 25 in the Year* 2000 (1976). This omission is the result not of cultural prejudice but of the existence of an interview with Berger, which is as informative as any discussion of mine could have been. It is reprinted in the appendix.

Geoff Dyer
Effra Hall, Brixton
January 1986

1. The 1950s

Marxism is so out of favour in Britain nowadays that to write about it at all may seem quaint.
Laurence Lerner 1956

Whenever I look at a work of art as a critic, I try — Ariadne like for the path is by no means a straight one — to follow up the threads connecting it to the early Renaissance, Picasso, the Five Year Plans of Asia, the man-eating hypocrisy and sentimentality of our establishment, and to an eventual socialist revolution in this country. And if the aesthetes jump at this confession to say that it proves that I am a political propagandist, I am proud of it. But my heart and eye have remained those of a painter.
John Berger 1956

It seems now that I was so near to that war.
I was born eight years after it ended. . .
Before I could see
Before I could cry out
Before I could go hungry

I was the world fit for heroes to live in.
(*W.B.* p.4)

John Berger was born into a world 'fit for heroes' on 5 November 1926. Eight years after another world war, in a world made safe for democracy, he was gaining some notoriety as an art critic. His initial career was shaped by the social convulsions of the Second World War and its aftermath.

Berger was 18 years old when the Labour Party swept to power with a massive majority and set up a welfare state that seemed to promise the arrival of something approaching socialism. Within three years, by 1948, the Labour government was running out of steam, uncertain what to do next. In 1950, their majority was almost wiped out and in the following year there began 13 years of Conservative rule. Far from being rooted in a fundamental shift of social consciousness, the legislative programme carried out by Labour did little more than cement the political consensus created by the pressures of war. When the Tories took office in 1951 they did not dismantle the welfare state but absorbed the optimistic energies which had been powerfully expressed in 1945. The post-war settlement and the development of consensual politics involved both of the major parties appealing to the same people on broadly similar terms; from the 1950s onwards, elections came to be decided by the floating votes of blue collar workers who did not see political choice in class terms. Laurence Kitchin wrote in 1960:

> It was not the State but the working class, having benefitted from wartime mobility and post-war legislation, which was withering away. Hunger, the prime mover of all radical politics, was no longer a major issue. It was soon to be replaced by galloping consumption and the era of organized greed.[1]

Keynesian capitalism had succeeded in regulating the economy, removing the spectre of mass unemployment and offering a steady increase in living standards for everyone – thereby undermining a central tenet of the labour movement: that capitalism was bound to lead to cycles of hunger and destitution. In the 1950s regulated free enterprise appeared to offer what socialists had claimed could only be achieved by public ownership. The 13 years of Conservative rule were less a product of Tory victory than of Labour's failure to bring about an ideological shift in the new constituency created by the war. The welfare state had relieved much of the pressure of poverty and hardship but that achievement provided the basis for the regeneration of capitalism and its expansion and invasion into hitherto undreamt of areas of peoples' lives.[2]

At the same time, this was the period of the Cold War. Conflict between East and West escalated in a string of events from the late 1940s onwards: the consolidation of communist power in Czechoslovakia and the Berlin blockade of 1948, the Soviet Union's first atomic bomb explosion in 1949, the Korean War of 1950–3, and later the Soviet invasion of Hungary. With only the model of the Soviet Union to look to, socialism became increasingly identified with totalitarianism. 'For ten years,' says Norman Broase in 1945 in Raymond Williams's *Loyalties*, 'communist has meant mainly anti–fascist. Within the next few years it will mean anti-liberal, anti-democratic, and then in practical terms subversive, even treasonable.' Cold War paranoia in Britain did not reach the depths it did in America, but to be remotely identified with communism was to be considered dangerous. (In 1949 the John Lewis Partnership ordered the dismissal of any employee who would not sign an anti-communist petition.)[3]

By the time Berger was 20 – and throughout the period described above – he considered himself a communist. As a boy he had been sent to a small preparatory school and then to St. Edward's in Oxford, an Anglo-Irish public school that aimed to produce minor colonial administrators and army officers. Both schools were savage and brutal, and at 16 he ran away from St. Edwards. He then gained a small scholarship and enrolled as a student at the Central School of Art. His adolescent political feelings had been anarchistic (he had read Kropotkin and other anarchist classics at school) but at Central he came into contact with a number of young communists and his political position hardened and became more clearly defined: less anarchist, more orthodox Marxist. His time at Central was cut short by his having to join the army where, because of his background, he was expected to take a commission. This he refused to do and so he was kept on as an instructor at the camp outside Belfast where he had been trained. The two years he spent there had a considerable effect on him. School had given him a sense of powerlessness in the face of bullying authority, but this was the first time he had had any real contact with working class men.

With a grant from the army he resumed his study of art – this time at the Chelsea – and became closely involved with the Communist Party (he wrote for their press and spoke on their platform but never became a member) and the Artists International Association (AIA). There were many influences on him at this time, defining and shaping his artistic and political outlook, but they can only be understood in the context of a more general consideration of art history as then practised and understood.

Broadly, art history has been dominated by methods which see the discipline in terms of a succession of individual artists, as a history of visual styles (i.e. formalism) or as part of a more general history of ideas (a kind of texts-and-contexts approach).[4]

These approaches do not necessarily set out their aims explicitly or rigidly. But tacit assumptions about art – assumptions concerning 'truth', 'beauty' and the nature of the creative genius which define what constitutes the fine art tradition – effectively seal off the

discipline of art history from actual historical and social relations.[5]
Such assumptions are inscribed in and passed on through the day-
to-day task of the critic, who occupies the influential middle
ground between academic experts and general public. In almost
identical terms, Roger Fry once claimed that he was 'a middle man
between the art historian and the amateur'– and the most influential critical method from the beginning of this century has
been the formalism associated with Fry and Clive Bell. 'What
quality is shared by all objects that provoke our aesthetic emotions?' asked Bell in 1914. His answer was 'significant form':
'lines and colours combined in a particular way, certain forms and
relations of forms'. Fry went on to make this notion central both
to an elaborately formulated theory of aesthetic effect and the criticism of contemporary art.

Also coming to the surface during the pre- and post-war years
of formalist supremacy, however, was a disparate body of Marxist-influenced writing on art and aesthetics with an emphasis on
the *social* history and social basis of art. The general work on
aesthetics was begun in the inter-war years by mid-European
theorists such as Lukács and the Frankfurt school (Horkheimer,
Benjamin, Adorno, Marcuse). In Britain in the 1930s there was no
comparable body of work (Christopher Caudwell was the only
major Marxist theorist of the Auden generation). The development of Marxist writing on the arts here, especially on the fine
arts, owes much to the arrival of European emigrés in the 1930s,
to the eventual dissemination of their ideas and to the publication
of their books in the 1950s and afterwards. Many of the artists,
scholars and communists that Berger came into contact with in the
late 1940s and early 1950s were emigrés who had fled from
fascism. Special mention must be made of one in particular: Frederick Antal.

Antal was born in Budapest in 1887 but worked in Florence,
Vienna and Berlin until he emigrated to England in 1933. Fluent
in several languages, an authority on fourteenth-century Italian
painting, Classicism, Romanticism and the English eighteenth
century, Antal was both expert and polymath. First published in
1938 in German, his *Florentine Painting And Its Social Background* (English edition 1948), like Arnold Hausser's *The Social
History Of Art* (published in English three years later, in 1951), is
a work of meticulous scholarly detail and grand historical sweep.
Here, Antal sets out the problem of defining 'style':

Considering each style as a combination of the specific elements of subject and form, the thematic elements offer an immediate transition to the general outlook on life, the philosophy from which the pictures in question derive. Works of art, considered thus are no longer isolated; we have penetrated beyond the formal and are touching upon something deeper, upon the conception of life. The formal elements, for their part, are in the final analysis also dependent upon the philosophies of the day, but the relationship is less direct and can be clearly discerned only after the primary consideration is understood, for the theme, the subject matter of the pictures shows more clearly than anything else how completely the picture as a whole is but a part of the outlook, the ideas of the public expressed through the medium of the artist. But the public is by no means unanimous in its outlook on life, and this divergence of outlook among its various sections explains the co-existence of different styles in the same period. Such divergence is, in its turn, due to the fact that what we call the public is not a homogenous body, but is split up into various often antagonistic groupings. Since the public is merely another word for society in its capacity as a recipient of art, what is required next is to examine the structure of society and the relationship between its various sections. To this end we must ascertain the economic and social causes which have produced these divisions. This should be our first concern for here we have solid ground under our feet. To sum up: we can understand the origins and nature of coexistent styles only if we study the various sections of society, reconstruct their philosophies and thence penetrate to their art.[6]

Even this excerpt is enough to show the extent to which Antal lays out the theoretical ground for the study of the social history of art. Yet his book is more widely dipped into than read, and more widely referred to than dipped into; the very thoroughness on which its reputation is based mitigates against its being read by a wide audience. In the 1950s Antal's work was known only to a small group of art historians, most of whom were hostile to it, and a small circle of Marxists. Berger became an unofficial pupil of Antal's and his influence on Berger, which was as much personal as theoretical, was enormous. Through Antal, the young Berger discovered a Marxism that was neither dogmatic nor philistine, an intellectual outlook more expansive and demanding than any associated with mainstream British art criticism. Years later, Berger remembered Antal as the person who 'more than any other man taught me how to write about art'. In the 1950s, Berger's was the most challenging critical voice in the art world and, while Antal remained virtually unknown, it was he who provided the theoretical backing for Berger's emerging critical project.

For Antal the AIA (in which he had been prominent since before the war) provided a forum where his work could link up with a wider artistic and political movement. Berger only became involved in the AIA at a time when its ideological strength was waning, but it is worth considering the history of the Association for two related reasons. First, because it serves as a link between the Popular Front of the 1930s and the Cold War of the 1950s and so helps us to see Berger's work in a developing historical context. Second, because many of the developments within it prefigure events and debates in which Berger played a principal role in the 1950s.

The Artists International Association was set up in 1933 as an alliance of artists specifically committed to a socialist political programme.[7] By 1936, while still an avowedly political organization, its objectives had broadened into part of a Popular Front 'against fascism and war and the suppression of culture'; membership had risen dramatically from just over 30 to more than 600, including some of the most prominent artists of the time. Fundraising exhibitions and activities continued throughout the Spanish Civil War, and as the Second World War approached, an Artists' Refugee Committee was formed to help people fleeing from fascism and Nazism. The ebullient years of the Association are recollected by James Fitton: 'Everyone was to the Left in those days. . . We were supported by everybody, people who normally would have voted High Tory'.

After the war and the defeat of fascism, that consensus collapsed. Economic crisis at home, successive crises in East-West relations and the widely reported Soviet criticisms of decadent modernist tendencies in music and art caused a split within the AIA between those who held to the original political objectives and those who saw the future of the Association in terms of an international but basically apolitical organization to aid artists. Sir Edward Marsh, Vanessa Bell and Duncan Grant resigned from the Advisory Council while Misha Black, a founder member, held that without the political clause in the constitution, the AIA 'could no longer hope to regain that position of intellectual leadership' which it had earned in the previous ten years. The political clauses were temporarily retained but the next three years, until 1953, were marked by uncertainty and caution.

The split within the AIA received its formal expression, so to speak, in 1952 with an exhibition of abstract and realist art entitled *The Mirror and the Square*. This marked a transitional stage between the traditional political role of the AIA and a new apolitical role. The exhibition effectively concealed a bitter ideological split by presenting 'only a formal confrontation of styles'. As soon as the debate was seen in terms of a conflict of styles – between realism and abstraction – it had effectively been lost by the political wing of the AIA who had claimed since the 1930s that realism was not simply an artistic style but 'an attitude to life, to the major social and political attitudes of [the] times'; now, instead, realism was simply 'one of numerous stylistic possibilities in contemporary art'.

In December 1953 a new version of the aims of the AIA was published. The original intention, 'to take part in political activity, to organize or collaborate in any meeting or demonstration in sympathy with the aims of the Association where action seems desirable or possible' was replaced by a new paragraph:

> To work for the co-operation of artists for intellectual freedom, economic security and the promotion of peace and international understanding; to organize or collaborate in any action for the above aims.

Ironically, in the twilight years of the AIA, a small revival of realist painting was taking place. In August 1950, the work of one of these young painters in an AIA exhibition of four new artists was singled out for attention by the *Manchester Guardian*. The painter was John Berger, whose work the reviewer wrote: 'faces outward towards the world more squarely, and his subjects – drunken fish- ermen, oxyacetylene welders, builders and acrobats – are reduced to a formal simplicity enclosed in thick black lines.' As Lynda Morris and Robert Radford have pointed out, Berger's work seemed to hark back to the everyday realism of the old days of the AIA and by so doing, it affirmed the Association's old values. His paintings were a direct extension of his political concerns. He spent six months in a foundry in Croydon, clocking in and out with the workers and sketching systematically; when the South Bank was being build for the Festival of Britain he went day after day to the building site and drew; later he spent four months on the coast of Brittany, sketching fishermen.

As well as continuing to work as an artist, teaching drawing and taking classes for the Workers' Educational Association, Berger gave radio talks on European masterpieces for the BBC West African Service. When he sent some of these scripts to the *New Statesman and the Nation* the editor, T.C. Worsley, asked him to do a review of an exhibition. That was in 1952; for the rest of the decade, Berger reviewed regularly for the *New Statesman*, fighting for realism in art and trying to establish the kind of art he himself had been producing.

A precedent to the approach to art which Berger encountered via the Communist Party and the AIA was set by Anthony Blunt, who reviewed for the *Spectator* in the 1930s. Though they were writing in different political climates, the arguments and phrases in Berger's reviews are remarkably similar to those of Blunt. Blunt, in Lynda Morris's phrase, saw 'the development of modern art as the progressive alienation of artists from all significant sections of society'.[8] He complained that Matisse's vision seemed 'no longer to be one of the real world', that Bonnard had turned to colour and form and away from 'human values', that the still life paintings of late Impressionism led away from serious issues 'to the various forms of esoteric and semi-abstract art which have flourished in the last century'. Abstract artists, he held, had cut themselves off 'from all the serious concerns of life' and were contented with dreams; it was the destiny of true art to find its way out of abstraction.

Blunt was also similar to Berger in what he praised. Rembrandt's honesty is 'so obvious that it strikes one as a moral quality', he wrote in 1938; he championed William Coldstream and turned towards the Mexican realist masters such as Rivera and Orozco as embodying the movement towards the future, 'helping the proletariat to produce its own culture'. Like Berger two decades later he held that 'the only hope for European painting at the present time is the development of a New Realism', that 'if art is a serious pursuit at all, it must be in some way related to the things which we think important in life', and that the artist 'should deal with the central realities of his period'. This is not to suggest that Berger was particularly influenced by Blunt, it is not even to suggest that he ever read these reviews; the important thing is that they shared the same formation; both of them were especially indebted to Frederick Antal.[9]

Berger's first reviews were unremarkable, but his distinctive strengths soon began to emerge: the painter's eye for light, the ability to evoke the effect of a picture in words, the concise formulation of compelling arguments. The writing in *Permanent Red*, a selection of articles from the 1950s, is startling. Although many books have their origins in essays or lectures, collections of short reviews are less usual and rarely impressive. What in a weekly or fortnightly column is an unnoticed expediency often reads, in book form, like hack work. The fact that *Permanent Red* reads as well as it does today is an indication of how outstanding was the work on which it was based.

Like all successful journalists, Berger was quick to learn to turn the limitations of space to his own advantage. His general technique throughout the 1950s is the one Raymond Williams noticed in Orwell: to assert, and then to argue *within that assertion*. It is essentially a combative style and early on, Berger set himself in opposition to established tastes; first by abruptly individual responses to individual painters (Francis Bacon is dismissed as 'a brilliant stage manager rather than an original visual artist') and then by enlarging on these judgements to call into question the consensus which these judgements opposed. 'I must admit', Berger wrote in January 1953, 'that as I read through what I have written in this journal during the last year, I realize how perverse many of my opinions and evaluations have been. By perverse, however, I only mean unfashionable: I find myself opposed to the general taste of most official and semi-official bodies.'[10] By the end of the decade, Berger was sufficiently confident of his own power to comment that the London art world was 'dominated by people who know nothing about art at all'.

Berger's acerbic tone is characteristic of a generation that briefly jolted the literary establishment in the mid 1950s. This establishment was made up of the heirs of the Bloomsbury group and the middle-aged survivors of the Auden generation, who had abandoned Marx and socialism in favour of a mild existentialism. Somehow, as Cyril Connolly noted in 1947, the 'left wing literary movement' had 'petered out'.[11] The atmosphere of the mid 1950s was 'of a conforming intellectual class as opposed to a dissenting one'.[12] Then a change took place, a change in attitude and tone rather than in politics. Reviews, as T.E.B. Howarth remarks a little wanly in his study of the 1950s, quite suddenly 'took on a new and waspish tone' in the middle years of the decade.[13] Kenneth Tynan, defender of *Look Back in Anger* and *Waiting for*

Godot, is the best remembered and one of the most perceptive of this new generation of iconoclastic young critics. He and Berger were friends and together with Penelope Gilliat (film critic of the *Observer*), they formed a young disruptive critical alliance as the Bloomsbury literary orthodoxy was shaken by the moment of angry young men.

Particularly among the young, the mood of the mid 1950s was one of disillusion, cynicism, frustrated idealism and emotional fatigue. The period was marked, as Lindsay Anderson (another friend of Berger's) wrote in 1956, by 'the steady draining away of vitality from what we may call the cultural left, its increasing modishness, and its more and more marked aversion to emotional simplicity or moral commitment.'[14] Disillusionment bred a jaded and impatient militancy, but since this militancy was rooted in the loss of faith that succeeded the ebullient promise of 1945 it could not find any outlet in political activity. The angry young men (often neither particularly angry nor young, sometimes not even men) were a contradictory, temporary phenomenon. At their centre was Jimmy Porter, whose 'people of our generation' speech in Osborne's *Look Back in Anger* still provides the favourite epigraph for any discussion of the period. In literature, the 'angry young man' label was extended to novelists like John Braine and merged into the other principal grouping of the 1950s, the poets of the so-called Movement. The link here was Kingsley Amis but other principle voices of the Movement – Philip Larkin and John Wain – were adamantly not angry.

In 1957, Tom Maschler edited *Declaration*, a collection of essays that has since acquired something of manifesto status for the contradictory and intemperate impulses of the angry young people. Contributors included Doris Lessing, Colin Wilson, Kenneth Tynan, Bill Hopkins, Lindsay Anderson, Stuart Holroyd and John Osborne. Kingsley ('I hate all this pharisaical twittering about the "state of our civilization" ') Amis refused to contribute. Of those who did, Anderson and Lessing were unequivocally on the left; as a whole, however, *Declaration* suggests that the angry young men movement is more usefully seen as an early manifestation of what developed into the 'generation gap' than as a sudden eruption of political radicalism.

Significantly, Berger was not asked to contribute to *Declaration*. The iconoclasm of the angry young men is emotional; despite its sincerity it lacks the ballast of responsibility. Jimmy Porter's tirades are powerful, fluent and incoherent; the intensity of his rage anticipates its exhaustion. There is an adolescent quality to much of the angry young men's anger that is appropriate to their egotism; they attack society as it affects them but leave its underlying logic unquestioned. The extent to which they depend on the social formation they attack points to a larger and more important contradiction. Trevor Blackwell and Jeremy Seabrook have pointed out that in the 1950s there took place 'an individualizing of socially produced phenomena' in which the individual was burdened with a weight of 'social and economic contradictions which [were] no longer articulated in public discourse'.[15] This is the phenomenon embodied in the angry young men. They were the product of an historical conjuncture (the post-war settlement) and responded to that conjuncture without any historical perspective and without acknowledging their debt to that history. Their anger both masked and was a product of their inability to understand historically their own position in the society they despised. Colin Wilson's *The Outsider* provides a metaphysical dimension to this sense of a historical displacement.

The subsequent development of the angry young men – the brevity of their anger – was already there as a condition of their existence. Historically, what is most characteristic of the angry young men is less the force of their conviction in the 1950s than the virtual unanimity of their move to the right in the decades following. In 1961 Osborne was reduced to writing a puerile letter of hate to his 'fellow countrymen':

You have instructed me in my hatred for 30 years. You have perfected it, and made it the blunt, obsolete instrument it is now. I only hope it will keep me going. I think it will. I think it may sustain me in the last few months.

Till then, damn you, England. You're rotting now, and quite soon you'll disappear. My hate will outrun you yet, if only for a few seconds. I wish it could be eternal.[16]

This was the last gasp of infantile radicalism before reaction set in.

Even earlier, in 1957, in a pamphlet called 'Socialism and the Intellectuals' Kingsley Amis complained of 'the flatulence of parlour marxism' and 'the irrational capacity to become inflamed by interests and causes that are not one's own'. He concludes that the intellectual has nothing 'to give the Labour movement'. A few months later *Labour Monthly* published an article pointing out that the disillusionment of the 1950s was not a product of hopes that were naive, but of hopes that were betrayed. Amis was castigated for his parochialism and for his lack of a world view which could serve as a working hypothesis for change. The article was by Berger, whose denunciations of the art world and the evils of privilege were always contained by exactly the kind of theoretical and political framework that the angry young men so blatantly disdained. Without such a framework, the angry young man of today was to become the conservative of tomorrow. Perhaps the abiding impression of the angry young men, in retrospect, is of their parochialism – they might not like England but they never look beyond it.

Berger's perspective, by contrast, was always global. He visited the Soviet Union in 1953 and wrote enthusiastically of his visit in the *New Statesman*. 'Until the Soviet Union gained nuclear parity', Berger has said in a recent interview, 'it was the victim of nuclear blackmail by the United States . . . at that moment, whatever your doubts, I felt you had to be *for* the Soviet Union.'[17] In his art criticism Berger was explicit about his political loyalties ('I am with the communists') and this made his position at the *New Statesman* precarious. In his introduction to *Permanent Red* he tells of having to fight for his copy 'line by line, adjective by adjective against constant editorial cavilling'. It was not until the last years of the decade, when Berger was protected by the personal support of Kingsley Martin, that he had more freedom.

Berger's declared political allegiances also gave his critics a ready weapon to use against him. Bryan Robertson, director of the Whitechapel Art Gallery complained that it was 'terrible to find views expressed on modern painting in the columns of the *New Statesman* which one would expected to find published within the narrower framework of the *Daily Worker*'. Further objections were not long in coming, and by the end of the decade some of the most influential voices in the cultural establishment had written in to the *New Statesman* to complain about its young art critic. Herbert Read declared, 'Bergerism is a post-Marxian heresy', while Stephen Spender remarked: 'Berger's criticism is like 'a foghorn in a fog'. (Berger wrote back to thank Spender for the compliment – what could be more useful in a fog than a foghorn, he wondered.) In the climate of the Cold War these criticisms were not surprising since although, as Robert Hewison remarks, 'bright-eyed, big-chested Stakhanovites painted in essentially nineteenth century academy style were not what Berger meant at all", [18] it was this Stalinist version of socialist realism that was immediately associated with the modified social realism supported by Berger against a conveniently (and sometimes crudely) defined abstraction. Although Berger always tried to couch his comments on abstract painting in terms of an unprejudiced response to particular examples of abstraction, the arguments he used to bolster that response always invite us to choose between two *kinds* of painting – one turned towards reality, the other in retreat from it. In 1954, Clement Greenberg was arguing persuasively against exactly the kind of prejudging of which Berger seemed guilty:

> To hold that one kind of art must invariably be superior or inferior to another kind means to judge before experiencing; and the whole history of art is there to demonstrate the futility of laws of preference laid down beforehand: the impossibility, that is, of anticipating the outcome of aesthetic experience.[19]

But Greenberg's argument is less convincing than it sounds since the nature of aesthetic experience is taken for granted.

The central debate in which Berger was involved throughout the 1950s comes back again and again to the nature of aesthetic experience – to the legitimacy or illegitimacy of certain kinds of response – and the terms in which it is relevant to consider that experience. However, this is to make Berger's critical project of the 1950s more abstract than it really was. The point is that this is the issue which, it can now be seen, lies behind his practical, active and gradually developing examination of the art of his time. More importantly, Berger's work has to be understood not only in terms of an argument within the art world but also in the light of the larger political context by which the realist/abstract debate is defined and to which it extends.

Berger's principal antagonist throughout the 1950s was Patrick Heron who also worked as an art critic for the *New Statesman*. Their first public squabble occurred in the Spring of 1953 when, for two months, the letters page of the *New Statesman* printed their Retorts Courteous, Replies Churlish, Reproofs Valiant and Counterchecks Quarrelsome. These were initiated by an aside from Heron that the 'return to realism' mentioned by Berger was no more than a fiction. For Heron, realism was 'that noble, disciplined straining to register with absolute objectiveness what the eye sees'; such realism, he went on, was rare in contemporary life. Berger wrote back arguing in the tradition of the AIA that realism depends 'upon the nature of conclusions drawn about the subject' and not upon the style of drawing. What Heron was talking about, said Berger, was naturalism. As for a developing realist movement in Britain – this was 'one of great potentiality rather than achievement'. Berger also took the opportunity to publish a personal declaration of his aims:

> If you only interpret art in terms of art (or purely visual experience), then the stylistic differences between, for example, Leger and Guttuso will blind you to their identity of aims. If, on the other hand, you try to interpret art in relation to life as a whole, it becomes obvious that both these painters belong to the significant number of European artists who are struggling, in the face of the obscurity and nihilism of so much contemporary work, to produce rational, constructive art which can comment upon, and express fairly objectively and with a sense of humane purpose, the development of the life they witness around them.[20]

This is a concise statement of an anti-formalist position which had been developed by the left over the previous decades. In the next issue of the magazine Heron replied, predictably, that 'art is autonomous' and that the road advocated by Berger inevitably led to a state where 'art and propaganda are one'. The controversy was fuelled by the appearance in the same issue of one of Berger's most notorious articles, a review of *The Unknown Political Prisoner*, a competition and exhibition organized by the Institute of Contemporary Arts (ICA). Berger's condemnation of the exhibition was an early attempt at the kind of argument he develops more fully in his essay 'Photographs of Agony' years later. The reason for the exhibition's failure, he wrote, stemmed from the belief that art should generalize, should be above and impartial to local, urgent, everyday issues: since we are implicated in the politics for which people are imprisoned, since the plight of the political prisoner is defined by an immediate political context, any attempt to treat the subject 'purely aesthetically' would betray it. The winning entry by Reg Butler was, Berger conceded, a compelling emblem of defeat but 'the fatal shortcoming of an emblem of defeat is that only a spectator, never a protagonist, can erect it'.[21]

This was the cue for everyone to climb in the ring and have their say. The next week the *New Statesman* printed a fraction of the mail it had received on the subject and 'the best part of four columns', as Berger emotively (and not entirely accurately) put it, were given over to 'personal attacks' on him. Naturally, things didn't stop there; next week it was Berger's turn. He wrote:

All my life I have been passionately concerned with painting. Besides practising as a painter, I have tried to think about and *for* art. But I have tried to think beyond the painter's brush; and, as a consequence, it has been my concern for art which has largely led to my general political and social convictions. Far from my dragging politics into art, art has dragged me into politics.[22]

In addition another whole page of letters from other people was given over to the subject, but the correspondence ended the following week (April 11, 1953) with a concluding manifesto from Heron. Art, Heron claimed, 'is in a vital sense autonomous. Art is spiritual discovery. Propaganda is the calculated injection of a dose of doctored facts. Art is permanent: propaganda is utterly ephemeral'.

No victor emerged from this quarrel; both Berger and Heron attacked parodies of each other's positions and neither, as Robert Hewison accurately puts it, 'managed to make [their] point sufficiently in terms of the other.'[23]* The sympathies of many readers of this book are likely to be with Berger rather than Heron but it has to be conceded that many of the former's attacks on abstract art were crude and ineffective. In the review of *The Unknown Political Prisoner*, Berger makes the point that 'shapes without meaning are not unlike sounds without words' – neglecting to add that sounds without words might be music rather than random cacophony. The problem, essentially, is that Berger seems to move constantly between using the phrase 'abstract art' to mean exactly that or as a shorthand for bad or poor abstract painting. His denunciation of abstract art as a whole is generated from a highly partial sample; based on the evidence of bad or poor abstract paintings his comments are presented as proof of the worthlessness of abstract art *per se*. At the same time, the fact that

* Berger and Heron had another lengthy epistolary clash a year later in March 1954, this time over the former's review of Henry Moore. Once again the letters page of the *New Statesman* was crammed with expressions of support and howls of outrage. The debate ended ironically when Victor Pasmore observed that by attacking Hepworth and Moore, Berger was really attacking modern art in general. In the same issue there appeared Berger's harsh review of an exhibition of Pasmore's own work.

his comments are about a particular kind or standard of abstract painting enables him to avoid the charge of pre-judging in terms of categories. Not surprisingly then, some of his comments are vague or contradictory. 'I am not anti-abstract', he wrote in 1952, 'I get considerable pleasure from those works in which real consideration lies behind each decision about colour and shape. The trouble is that the pleasure is incomplete'. In the same article, he complained of abstract art which interprets reality without investigating it, which is involved with 'sensations and feelings that are never "earthed" '.[24] What is meant by 'earthed' is not clear – its meaning is not 'earthed' – but the choice of word reveals how insistently Berger comes back to the tangible, the real – from which abstract painting is felt to be a turning away, offering instead 'an entirely contemplative world', 'a refuge for the privileged'. For Berger, what abstract paintings leave out always beckons more urgently than what is displayed on the canvas. What abstract paintings lack is significant *content* – content which, as he wrote in an essay on Barbara Hepworth, can only be derived 'from definite, specific, particular experience'. We do not have to look very far in Berger's own writings to see how untenable this line of reasoning is. Content, Berger stresses again and again, is not subject matter. Content is subject matter *worked on*, not what the subject is but *how* the artist sees it: 'content is what the artist discovers and emphasizes in his subject matter'.[25] By this time the door is already wide open for abstraction: the artist may look at something – anything – and what he or she discovers in it may be *formal* perfection. As Leger says, 'If I isolate a tree in a landscape, if I approach that tree, I see that its bark has an interesting design and a plastic form; that its branches have dynamic violence which ought to be observed; that its leaves are decorative.'[26]

Additionally, since for Berger, content – that which is discovered in a subject – is the crucial element, paint itself can be the subject of a painting; what matters is how intensely it has been worked, what the artist discovers in his or her medium. Meaning, in other words, can be expressed and understood formally – a point which, as Michael Armstrong shows, Berger implicitly concedes in his discussions of such painters as Piero and Poussin who are remote from the polemical urgencies of the present.[27] As he later has Lavin say in *A Painter of our Time*: 'every formal quality has its emotional equivalent', has, in other words emotive content – and it is really the quality of this emotive content that preoccupies Berger. He responds warmly to Matisse whose 'reds, blacks, golds, ceruleans flow over the canvas with the strength and yet utter placidity of water above a weir, the forms carried along on their current because his colours express 'the nearly religious feeling' he has towards 'sensuous life'.[28] Berger is at pains to point out that these 'pure colours' are not abstract (note the way that he establishes a link between pure colour and the objective world through the 'water above a weir' simile) because they serve expression. (But this is a red herring: how can *colours* be either *abstract* or *non-abstract*? Are not Rothko's huge 'empty' canvases both abstract and expressive?) Relatedly, in the cases of non-abstract artists like Henry Moore and Francis Bacon, Berger's objections are essentially responses to the *emotive content* of their work. Moore's is 'the very opposite of a work that aspires'; Bacon's Pope 'screams not because of the state of his conscience or the state of the world but, puppet-like, because he has been put into Bacon's glass-case'. (This argument obviously anticipates the later objection that in Bacon 'the worst is assumed to have already taken place'.) Art dominated by the artist's despair, contends Berger, becomes solipsistic and therefore trivial since it is 'blind to the fact that the whole world is being changed by the vigour of millions determined to enjoy the advantages and rights of a technical, humanist civilization.'[29] The artist's despair is a denial of history, a reactionary preoccupation with state at the expense of process.

The emotional equivalent of much abstract painting is seen by Berger as a kind of hysterical splurging, a wild splashing in all directions at once – a practice canonized by the abstract expressionists or 'action' painters and negatively contrasted with Mondrian who 'by the 1940s had pioneered abstract art to its limits'. Since Mondrian, the only way to take abstract art further, wrote Berger, was to introduce 'an arbitrary emotionalism which he [Mondrian] would have hated with all possible fervour'.[30]

Mondrian, according to Berger, achieved his unparalleled 'tautness' and 'spring' by destroying nine-tenths of himself in order 'to pack the final tenth with phenomenal vitality'. Berger comes back frequently to these ideas of discipline, control and organization at a time when action painting (the phrase was first coined by Harold Rosenberg in 1952) offered an unencumbered liberation from these qualities in favour of a spontaneous eruption whose arbitrary logic could (or could not) be recognized later. In contrast to Leger's delight in 'the architecture of the mechanical' and Mondrian's disciplined vitality, Berger saw the abstract expressionists as representatives of a culture that was disintegrating into trivia and despair. In 1949, Cyril Connolly had predicted that 'from now on an artist will be judged only by the resonance of his solitude or the quality of his despair.'[31] For Berger, 'Abstract expressionism, "action" painting or whatever you like to call it . . . is the most literal reflection of the ultimate, passive hopelessness of *laissez faire*; the subjective justification of what has happened as the result of almost pure accident.'[32] Earlier in the same year he wrote that the works of the action painters, 'in their creation and appeal, are a full expression of the suicidal despair of those who are completely trapped within their own dead subjectivity'. In 1958, he sees 'this kind of non-art' seen as reflecting 'unconsciously and passively a reality: the reality of the fears, the cynicism, the human alienation that accompanies the death throes of imperialism'.

It is as though the vehemence of Berger's attack on action painting finally led him to temper his initially indiscriminate rejection of it. By rejecting the aesthetic emphasis on painterly gesture and stressing that action painting embodied a larger process of disintegration and nihilistic abandonment, whose most vivid symbol is the atom bomb, Berger ended up granting a significance to it that he set out to deny. In other words, action paintings may be meaningless as art but the way in which they are meaningless is significant. This is his position in the essay on Jackson Pollock in *Permanent Red*. The essay's conclusion offers a verdict on Pollock's work and the dialectical resolution of Berger's own arguments:

> If a talented artist cannot see or think beyond the decadence of the culture to which he belongs, if the situation is as extreme as ours, his talent will only reveal negatively but unusually vividly the nature and extent of that decadence. His talent will reveal, in other words, how it itself has been wasted. (*P.R.* p.70)

'The drive towards realist painting in the early 1950s', claims Robert Hewison, 'was largely the work of one man, John Berger, whose political views over-emphasized the ideological aspect of realism and probably did the movement some harm.'[33] This second contention is open to question; the first is inaccurate. In fact, between 1952 and 1956, in articles and exhibitions, artists and critics were embroiled in a debate about the nature, purpose and value of the increasing numbers of realist paintings that were being produced.[34] Berger's rise to prominence in the 1950s would not have been possible without the widespread interest in and importance of the issues raised by the debate in which he was involved.

'In 1952', wrote David Sylvester a year later, 'the London art world revealed a growing obsession with the contentious issue of whether a return to realism in painting was desirable or possible'.[35] Berger's *Looking Forward* exhibition at the Whitechapel in September was only one of three important realist exhibitions held in that year (the others were *Five Young French Realists* at the Arcade Gallery and *Recent Trends in Realist Painting* organized by Robert Melville, Peter Watson and Sylvester himself). The exhibition organized by Berger had a specific aim:

> That aim is to show the work of painters who draw their inspiration from a comparatively objective study of the actual world: who inevitably look at a subject through their own personality but who are more concerned with the reality of that subject than with the 'reality' of their feelings about it.[36]

The young realists in the exhibition, claimed Berger, look forward to the time when artists will again be able to communicate beyond an artistic elite. Two of the painters in the exhibition soon became prominent: Jack Smith and Derrick Greaves. John Bratby, not included in Berger's exhibition but championed by him, also held a one-man show at the Beaux Art Gallery in Bruton Street. In 1956 the three were selected to represent Britain at the Venice Biennale; the realists, as Basil Taylor of the *Spectator* put it, had 'received their certificate of official approval'.[37] The drive towards realist painting was not, then, the work of one man. What other commentators found it difficult to share was Berger's attempt to define realism in political terms. As far as Sylvester was concerned, Berger had contributed 'some thoroughly doctrinaire leftish articles' to the *New Statesman*. Even some of the realist artists themselves were unhappy at being appropriated for political ends.[38] Jack Smith, one of the artists that Berger championed, published a letter in the *Listener* in 1955, disassociating himself from social realism.

From the start, Berger was at pains to distinguish between realism and naturalism, that 'thoughtless, superficial goggling at appearances'.[39] He was also at pains to distinguish between social realism and socialist realism: social realism exists where 'the content of a realist work has clear social implications' and these implications exist irrespective of whether the artists themselves have definite political or social views. Socialist realism on the other hand depends on the artist being 'militantly aware of the social implications of what he is doing . . . his attitude will then be active instead of passive and the ideas of striving and achievement will be more stressed in his work.' He goes on to warn about the dangers of using art to forward a political programme:

> To demand, however, that [young social realists] should be aware in this way would at the moment be premature, because such militancy is outside their experience and theoretical militancy only produces forced propaganda. As it is, the fact that they can find heroic inspiration only in the lives of those denied security, reveals the frustration of spirit behind the apathy and comparative comfort of the welfare state, and in accepting this inspiration they are brave prophets.[40]

In distinguishing between realism and naturalism, Berger, throughout the 1950s, drew heavily on the vocabulary and ideas of Georg Lukács. Lukács's writing on realism concentrated almost solely on the novel and Berger 'translated' his insights from literature to art. For Lukács, realism was a realization through fictional characters of actual historical forces. The 'typical' character was one whose actions and circumstances defined and embodied the sociohistoric forces of which he or she was a part. Naturalism on the other hand represents meticulously observed detail drained of historical meaning. The naturalist describes passively, the realist actively creates a complex historical whole, his work grasps the 'world-historical forces of an epoch that make for change'. The realist reaches the historical essence of society; the naturalist is content with the surface. For Lukács the point at which realism declined into naturalism (in the novel) was 1848 – the year of failed revolutions – when the progressive momentum of the bourgeoisie gave way to oppressive consolidation of their power. That is the crucial year, separating the realist achievements of Tolstoy and Balzac from the naturalism of Flaubert and Zola. Lukács is not simply distinguishing between two methods of writing – or between pairs of writers who, as individuals, are simply better or worse writers than each other – but between two historically determined possibilities: for Lukács, after 1848 the conditions did not exist for the production of great realist works. In advocating a return to realism, then, was Berger simply hoping for a transhistorical journey across time as well as across disciplines? Terry Eagleton describes the 'disintegration' noticed by Lukács in these terms:

> Individuals are gripped by despair and *angst*, robbed of social
> relations and so of authentic selfhood; history becomes
> pointless or cyclical, dwindled to mere duration. . . If
> naturalism is a kind of abstract objectivity, formalism is an
> abstract subjectivity; both diverge from the genuinely
> dialectical art form [realism] whose form mediates between
> concrete and general, essence and existence, type and
> individual.[41]

This sounds exactly like the kind of process Berger felt he was
living through in the 1950s. In other words, Berger was arguing
for a return to realism at a moment in history strikingly similar to
that moment more than a century earlier, when realist ambitions
became impossible to achieve and had, of necessity, to dwindle
into the diminished expectations of formalism and naturalism.

Lukács was not, of course, an infallible guide to the past or a
prophet of the future. Berger's analysis and hopes were contradictory only within Lukács's logic, and only for as long as we accept the Lukácsian postulates on which they are based. The important point is itself historical: by the end of the decade nothing
remained of the realist movement in painting that Berger had
championed for almost ten years; it was US abstract expressionism that had 'won' in the market. In October 1959, in an
article stoically entitled 'Staying Socialist' Berger conceded that
'nowhere in Western Europe is there a realist stronghold left.'[42]
The article confirms what had been negatively and implicitly evi-
dent in Berger's criticism for a number of years. Impatience with
the works he was reviewing, an increasingly explicit contempt for
those who organized exhibitions, an increasing sense of the art of
the time being contaminated by a more general disintegration – in
short, the sheer number of hostile reviews (including attacks on
Bratby and Smith whom he had previously championed) that he
wrote indicated that the healthy return to realism had not taken
place. Clearly, somewhere, he had made a mistake.

As Berger saw it at the time, the mistake lay in misunderstand-
ing 'the contemporary social role of the visual arts in Western
Europe' where other means of communication – television,
cinema, drama – had become more effective. As a direct means of
communication, the visual arts, by comparison, were 'very ineffi-
cient'. Technological advance, the blunting of visual awareness
through what seemed like a bombardment of sensational images,

'the narrow laboratory atmosphere' in which the great visual in-
novators worked and the 'total economic dependence of the artist
on the bourgeoisie' went hand in hand with a social base of the visual arts that had shrunk to the point where they could not contain
the broad scope of which Berger hoped they were capable. What
Berger had prophesied in painting was, however, occurring in
other areas of communication; in literature, drama and television.
Berger noted that works such as *The Lambeth Boys, Look Back In
Anger, The Kitchen* and *Room At The Top* satisfied 'many of my
often repeated critical demands'.

After reaffirming his belief in a general Marxist analysis of the
arts, Berger goes on to offer some new reflections on realism and
from these comes the definition of realism preserved in the pages
of *Permanent Red*. As in the Pollock essay, this passage represents
the resolution of difficulties and contradictions which had
been actively worked through in the previous ten years. Social and
socialist realism are brought together in the interests of a socialist
humanism which looks forward to Berger's work in the next decade:

> Realism can only be defined within a given situation. Its
> methods and aims are always changing. . . The realist must look
> at the modern world . . . and come to terms with it. That is to
> say he has got to answer the question – What is man? A
> question which, as Gramsci pointed out, really means: What
> can man become? Up to about 1920, artists could answer this
> question confidently enough without necessarily being
> socialists. Since then, if they are to reach a satisfactory answer,
> socialism has become increasingly necessary for them.
> (*P.R.* pp. 208-9)

In an essay in the catalogue of *The Forgotten Fifties* exhibition,
Berger looked back on the efforts of himself and others who tried
to bring about the realist revival: 'Our weaknesses were due to our
isolation – both geographical and ideological. We were too alone
and in the long run we didn't have enough confidence. Above all,
we were too impatient.' The geographical and the ideological are
closely related: Berger's enthusiasm for realist art was fuelled by
the powerful realist movements in France and (especially) Italy
where the realists had been given a salon at the 25th Venice Biennale in 1950 – six years before Bratby and others represented Britain. (Incidentally, Berger's first book, published in translation in

Dresden in 1953 and then in Moscow but still unpublished in Britain, was a study of the greatest Italian Social Realist, Renato Guttuso.) In France and Italy, where the development of realism was inseparable from the fight against fascism, the realist movements came out of the war with strong political roots. The realist movement in Britain – as can be seen in the story of the AIA – emerged from the war without anything like the same political thrust and so the movement was inadequately underwritten by a supporting ideology. Realism, as Morris and Radford put it, flourished for a few years in post-war England 'as the latest art movement divorced from social or political issues.'[43]

Berger was also suffering at the hands of British cultural history. In Britain there was no 'tradition' of Marxist modernism as there had been in Europe. Significantly a slogan of the AIA was 'Radical in Politics, Conservative in Art'. The possibility of a modernist radicalism simply did not exist; the ideological accompaniment of English modernism had already been determined by those like T.S. Eliot who held that modern art had to be difficult, elusive and elitist. In the 1950s, realism represented the only possible option for the left; Berger's attempts to define realism more imaginatively than had hitherto been the case indicated an awareness of the need to broaden and build from this option. This polarization was a product of the Cold War; in defending realism against Abstract Expressionism, Berger was intuitively aware that he was resisting US cultural hegemony. He was not alone in this. Paul Hogarth in 1955 in the *Marxist Quarterly* wrote:

> We know that the economic effects of rearmament are fundamentally responsible for the drastic economies that were made in expenditure on education and culture, in the budgets of Labour and Tory governments. We know the effects it had on rents, food prices, a seat at the cinema and concert. But it should also be known how rearmament and cold war thinking affected the nature of art itself.[44]

The extent to which this was the case has only recently become apparent. After the war, US economic, political and cultural influence increased massively. The unremitting anti-Soviet propaganda of the 1950s was an attempt to consolidate this power and resist, as far as possible, the growing might of the Soviet Union. 'We must not be confused about the issue which confronts the world today – it is tyranny against freedom', President Truman had said in 1948 and during the period of his administration (despite Truman's personal antipathy to avant garde art) art became a weapon in this struggle. The Soviet cultural bureaucracy imposed a strict discipline of socialist realism on its artists (Zhdanovism); Abstract Expressionism, the developing art movement in America, on the other hand, was characterized by impulses exactly opposed to the rigid discipline of Soviet realism. Within America, Abstract Expressionism triumphed because, the work itself 'coincided fairly closely' with the ideology of 'new liberalism' that dominated American political life after 1948 presidential elections.[45] Internationally, the unfettered art of Abstract Expressionism was a highly suitable vehicle for propagating an ideology of free expression against restrictive Soviet artistic practice. Wherever possible, the Museum of Modern Art (MOMA) and the US Information Service championed Abstract Expressionism. Moreover, as Peter Fuller remarks:

> The CIA was also active in the inflation of the alleged 'triumph' of Abstract Expressionism: Thomas W. Braden, a former MOMA executive secretary, supervized CIA cultural activities in the early 1950s. He admitted that enlightened members of the bureaucracy fully realized the propaganda value of marshalling 'dissenting opinions' within 'the framework of agreement on Cold War fundamentals'. Braden and his colleagues, wherever possible, supported the avant garde rather than the 'realists'.[46]

The effect of this cultural expansion (together with the rise in art prices by which it was accompanied) was to shift the centre of artistic creation from Europe (especially Paris) to New York; in England, as Fuller concludes, 'a weak, indigenous Fine Art tradition was effectively swamped'.

More generally, Berger was *for* a reintegration of art and society as part of a larger political project at a time when technological and social changes were causing art to become increasingly self-determining, increasingly grounded in its own logic. As Harold Rosenberg continually pointed out, the virtually 'universal pictorial vocabulary' of the 1960s had been evolving since the Second World War. Instead of working from within a single tradition from the past, says Rosenberg, stylistic affiliations were beginning to be chosen from 'among possible futures'.[47] In an age of mass reproduction an array of stylistic options were available independent of the circumstances that brought them into being. In choosing an artistic style an artist, as it were, begins the future rather than continues the past. All the interest is on what happens next. This development in art was paralleled by developments in the growing market for consumer durables. Both trends did not gather their full momentum until the 1960s but by the end of the previous decade, Berger was already experiencing the first rumblings of changes which lead to an increasingly central theme in his work: the way that 'what-is-to-come, what-is-to-be-gained empties what-is'. Significantly, in 1956, an exhibition of Pop Art entitled *This is Tomorrow* was held at the Whitechapel Gallery. The contrast in title between that exhibition and Berger's own *Looking Forward* of a few years previously was indicative of a larger transition 'from socialist planning to the hire purchase promise that you can enjoy the future now.'[48]

The 1950s, then, did not represent a moment of historical convergence adequate or 'intense' enough to bring about the return to realism that Berger hoped for. This is clear to us now (as Philip K. Dick once said, 'this is the famous nature of hindsight: to it everything is inevitable, since everything has already happened') in a way that it was not to Berger at the time; he was trying to shape the history in which he was situated and in some important respects he succeeded. Ernst Fischer commented in 1959:

> Any ruling class which feels threatened tries to hide the *content* of its class domination and to present its struggle to save an outdated *form* of society as a struggle for something 'eternal', unassailable, and common to all values. Hence the defenders of the bourgeois world do not speak today of its capitalist content but of its democratic form, though this form is cracking at every joint.[49]

This tendency to overlook content, Fischer continues, 'has brought into being the phenomenon of "formalism" in the sphere of the arts'. The question of formalism in the arts, then, is not confined to questions of artistic expression but is part of a larger political 'emphasis laid on form as though it were the essential thing'.

Berger was not only asserting the importance of content over form in art, he was also implicitly raising the stakes for the discussion of art in a popular and politically influential periodical. Questions about art, because of the way he argued them through, led automatically to questions of society. Berger in the 1950s played a vital part in transforming public discussion of art from a marginal discussion of *form* – of something separate from the political life of society – into something which not only had a vital connection *with* but was an essential part *of* the content of that society. Earlier I claimed that Berger's work in the 1950s comes back again and again to a contestation of the nature of aesthetic experience, to the legitimacy or illegitimacy of certain kinds of.response, even though his argument was rarely articulated in terms as abstract as these. It should be clear by now that this question was anything but abstract: throughout the decade Berger was aware of what Harold Rosenberg wrote later, that 'choices having to do with method in art become in practice attitudes regarding the future of man'.[50] In the 1950s, Berger turned these choices into a battle and embodied 'attitudes' in concrete political terms.

2. Transition

The political intellectual is concerned with the institutional life of the society: the creative artist with the attitudes, the manners, the moral and emotional life which the individual consummates within that social framework. It seems to me that the beginning of a common socialist humanism is the realization that these are not two distinct areas of interest but the complementary parts of a complex, common experience.
Stuart Hall, 1958

In one sense, Berger's error of prophecy was a vindication of his method: he was right in stressing the social forces that work on art, wrong in his understanding of how they were working in this particular instance. He was, if you like, being proved generally right in the process of being proved particularly wrong. As early as 1953 he had written: 'The more I think about the definitions and problems relevant to the position of the artist today, the more convinced I become that they cannot be resolved in terms of art'.[1] Nor could they be dealt with by the analytical equipment he had to hand. There was a clear need to develop a method of analysis which, in the terms Raymond Williams was later to develop, situated art within the whole complex process of actual and active social relations. On the one hand this meant lengthier, more detailed work; on the other, work with a broader cultural and historical sweep. Either way, Berger had gone as far as he could in the context of short, fortnightly reviews. In 1959 he published the articles which form the introduction to *Permanent Red* and which represent the fullest working out of the problems he had grappled with for the previous seven years. Proper criticism, says Berger, must ask: 'What can art serve here and now?' More precisely, the question he asks in front of a particular painting is: 'Does this work help or encourage men to know and claim their social rights?' By that, Berger goes on to explain, he does not mean that art should be preoccupied with the justice of a social cause; what he does mean 'is something less direct and more comprehensive':

> After we have responded to a work of art, we leave it, carrying away in our consciousness something which we didn't have before. This something amounts to more than our memory of the incident represented, and also more than our memory of the shapes and colours and spaces which the artist has used and arranged. What we take away with us – on the most profound level – is the memory of the artist's way of looking at the world. The representation of a recognizable incident (an incident here can simply mean a tree or a head) offers us the chance of relating the artist's way of looking to our own. The forms he uses are the means by which he expresses his way of looking. The truth of this is confirmed by the fact that we can often recall the experience of a work, having forgotten both its precise subject and its precise formal arrangement.
>
> Yet why should an artist's way of looking at the world have any meaning for us? Why does it give us pleasure? Because, I believe, it increases our awareness of our own potentiality. Not of course our awareness of our potentiality as artists ourselves. But a way of looking at the world implies a certain relationship with the world, and every relationship implies action. (*P.R.* p.18)

Two categories of work offer this promise of increased potential: those which 'embody a way of looking that promises a mastering of reality', and those whose promise lies in 'the fervour of an implied desire for change'. He concludes by pointing out that the meaning of a work of art changes, depending on 'what obstacles are impeding human progress at any given time'. Therefore:

> It is our century, which is pre-eminently the century of men throughout the world claiming the rights of equality, it is our own history that makes it inevitable that we can only make sense of art if we judge it by the criterion of whether or not it helps men claim their social rights. It has nothing to do with the unchanging nature of art – if such a thing exists. (*P.R.* p.18)

With that essay, Berger's work for the *New Statesman* effectively came to an end. It was the high point of his work as a regular art critic, the point from which his work would develop and to which it would most frequently refer back.

Written in the same year but not published until 1961 in *Labour Monthly*, 'Problems of Socialist Art' is a closely related article that contains in fairly developed form what would become his main concerns, themes and methods in writing on art.[2] Anticipating his work on Picasso and Cubism, Berger asks, 'how do we regard the art produced in or around Paris between about 1870 and 1920?' He poses the central question of *Ways of Seeing*: 'Have any of us yet fully worked out how the social function of painting has been changed by the inventions and developments of other media?' More generally he wonders how art can 'play its part in creating the new socialist man? What is the *social* function of art?'

In his endeavours to answer this question we can see the influence of Ernst Fischer, whom Berger visited in Vienna in 1961. Fischer was born in Austria in 1899, he joined the Communist Party in 1934 and from then until after the war 'step by step . . . became persuaded of the correct policy, the historical greatness of Stalin, the grandeur of his work'.[3] Subsequently, he repudiated Stalinism and *The Necessity of Art* develops a humanist conception of art in strict opposition to Zhdanovism. (His later book, *Art Against Ideology*, as the title suggests, takes an even stronger oppositional line.) Art, anticipating humanity's eventual restoration under communism, says Fischer, 'can raise man up from a fragmented state into that of a whole', and 'restore the lost unity of man'. More to the point, Fischer's book thoroughly worked through the distinctions between form and content, and definitions of naturalism and realism that Berger had been grappling with for the previous decade. Fischer had lived through the political consequences of his thought; his book appeared to Berger both as a vision of what he could achieve and of the immensity of the labours that still lay ahead.

It is no accident that Fischer, like many of Berger's mentors or guides, was a European. For much of the 1950s, Berger had travelled abroad and in 1960 he left England for good. His reasons for leaving were complex and personal; on different occasions he has emphasized different motives. The essential point is that he found England stifling; there was no place for him there. In France, on the other hand, 'there were people working . . . whom I felt close to: Sartre; in a different way, Camus; Merleau-Ponty. In the Britain that I left there were no thinkers like that.'[4] Above all he wanted to change his role from critic to creative writer, or, more exactly, to have the freedom to write what he wanted. This shift was already implicit in his criticism. In 1955 he had written that 'the true function of a critic is not that of an impresario but that of a poet and thinker combined' – a grandiose but prophetic description of what he would later become. His most illuminating comments on criticism and his own development were in a review of Baudelaire's *The Mirror of Art*:

> Behind all creative criticism – as opposed to technical or biographical analysis – there is doubt and a tragic contradiction ... great creative criticism only occurs when a hope, a theory of art, promises more than the practice of it, when the writer has a vision of art in his mind which no painting, nor poem, nor song can altogether equal in largeness, generosity, brilliance... In all great criticism one finds the vision of a New State, and yet not a brick laid towards directly building it.[5]

Hence the critic's doubts and contradictions: with all this talent why does he criticize instead of create? If the aim is to improve lives then why not write about politics instead of art? These are the doubts, says Berger, that appear between every line of the theories of art of Tolstoy, Baudelaire, Ruskin and Morris; each of them turned to art because 'it was the most obvious noble constant of all history, as the field in which to build his individual vision of a better future'. For these writers 'criticism became the shadow *preceding* the body'.

The greatness attributed to the critics of the past is the embodied expression of his own gradually shaping ambitions; their doubts – 'if he has so much imagination and energy, why does he not preserve it for his own actual creations?' – are Berger's. With its emphasis on criticism – on *creative* criticism – as the shadow preceding the body, Berger outlines his own hopes for his future.

While his or her sole outlet is criticism, the talented writer is frequently tempted to draw attention to the creative effort involved in critical endeavour. For Berger there has rarely been any real distinction between the two activities; criticism for him requires scarcely less imaginative effort than any other kind of writing. All his writing is criticism in the sense, noted by Barthes, of *bringing into crisis*. His leaving England should thus be seen as part of a project to throw off a socially perceived role rather than as a leap between two distinct literary practices; the actual 'transition' from criticism to creative writing was easily done.

Berger's ability to move almost unconsciously between different forms of writing and between disciplines is partly a comment on his talent (and is related, almost certainly, to his having avoided the specialization of formal academic training) but it is also related to the opportunities for publication and literary development that came his way. The sharp division between different kinds of writers in our society – and the tendency of writers to specialize, to write only on sport, or jazz, or whatever – has more to do with the way that such divisions are institutionalized and perpetuated by the rigid allocation of space for particular purposes than it has to do with the limitations of individual writers. Berger's exceptional discursive mobility is as much an indication of his *success* as a writer as it is of his talent. His work throughout the 1960s and 1970s has appeared in a variety of magazines and newspapers, but Berger's variety of writing could not have been achieved without the particular opportunities afforded by the format and editorial policy of *New Society*. Being a writer is inseparable from having the *chance* to be a writer, and that is as true for great writers as it is for anyone else.

In an objectionable introduction to the Picador edition of the book that shot him to fame, Colin Wilson recalled how: 'When *The Outsider* appeared, T. S. Eliot told me that I had achieved recognition the wrong way; it was fatal to become known to too many people at once. The right way was to gradually achieve an audience of regular readers, and slowly expand from there, if at all.' In his work for the *New Statesman*, Berger had built up exactly this audience of regular readers. Many of them must have been eager to read more by him and this probably gave his publishers the confidence to publish his novels (as it equally probably gave Berger the confidence to write them). His first novel, closely related to his art criticism, is a masterpiece; his next two, unmitigated failures.

3. A Painter of our Time

My duty was dictated by history itself.
Victor Serge

Janos Lavin, the painter, looks at his finished canvas *The Games* and reflects on the way that: 'What is most striking about it today may seem irrelevant in 20 years' time. This abundance of the artist's intentions is what makes the problem of propaganda so complicated. Nevertheless, it is *the* problem of art in our time.' (*P.T.* p.142) This is exactly the critical dilemma posed by Berger's first novel. As we shall see, it is the novel's precise location in the events of its time that led to its being withdrawn soon after publication and which, paradoxically, guarantees its continuing importance today.

The novel opens in classic mystery tradition with the narrator, John, letting himself into the studio of a friend who has disappeared. The place is eerily quiet with 'an accumulated absence of sound'. Brushes have stiffened in jars of turps; palette knives crusted in paint have been left lying around. On the draining board there is a pot with the tea still in it; an unwashed cup. As he pokes around the studio John comes across 'broken plates' and 'a broken bucket' – fragments of the past that he cannot decipher – photographs, a torn piece of paper with MAY I OFFER YOU MY HEARTFELT CONGRATULATIONS written on it, scraps of paper that he looks at 'in the vague hope that they would give me a clue to what I had not known, to what I had missed.'

Objects acquire meaning through use, from our touching and moving them. Hence the slight shock we feel when we arrive back somewhere after a period of absence and find that everything is as it was but somehow different:

> Look at the pictures and the cutlery.
> The music in the piano stool. That vase.[1]

Spilled paint has formed a skin on the table where John's friend, the painter Janos Lavin, had worked. In Lavin's studio, meaning has congealed. A few minutes later, John accidentally comes across Lavin's journal but its contents, written in Hungarian, make little sense. It is only when a friend translates it for him that he realizes, as Berger announces with characteristic directness, that the journal amounts to 'a *Portrait of the Artist as an Emigré*, and today in one sense or another most artists are *emigrés*'.

The novel is made up principally of extracts from this journal, linked by John's commentary. If the book had consisted solely of the journal, and if Lavin had been an actual artist, then it would have to be considered as one of the vital source documents of twentieth century art. There are the observations on other artists:

> This was Michelangelo's secret as much as it is Leger's. It is the energy of their bodies that fills their faces with meaning. It is the opposite of Rembrandt. In Rembrandt, it is the expression that gives the body meaning. Moreover, by expression in that sense we always mean tragic expression. Happiness is curiously impersonal. (*P.T.* p.125)

There is Berger's extraordinary sensitivity to light and colour:

> There are two types of colour: apparent colour and actual colour. Apparent colour – the colour of the sky, the sea, sunlight on earth, shadow on flesh or any object in light – always imply within themselves the victory of the colour they present over all other possible colours. Somewhere on the blue-black of a night sky there is a vanquished red, a vanquished green, even a vanquished yellow. We have to create this vibrancy not separately in each colour we apply, but through the relationship one to another of the colours we use on each canvas. In terms of colour we have to transform depth into breadth. (*P.T.* p.130)

There is the ability to convey, as few other books on artists have been able to, the actual daily labour of an artist. 'Separate the idea of fire from the fact of fuel', wrote Berger of Minelli's film of Van Gogh, *Lust For Life*, 'and you are left with a miracle'.[2] Berger's novel *A Painter of our Time* is dominated by the fact of fuel. It is about a painter rather than paintings, about 'the studio defeats and victories which make up a large part of the painter's life'; it is about the addictive, exhausting routine of a lifetime of self-discipline, 'the slave-driving necessity to work', the urge to return again and again to the unfinished work. Raymond Carver has memorably expressed this in his poem 'Balzac':

> I think of Balzac in his nightcap after
> thirty hours at his writing desk,
> mist rising from his face,
> the gown clinging
> to his hairy thighs as
> he scratches himself, lingers
> at the open window.
> Outside, on the boulevards,
> the plump white hands of the creditors
> stroke moustaches and cravats,
> young ladies dream of Chateaubriand
> and promenade with the young men, while
> empty carriages rattle by, smelling
> of axle-grease and leather.
> Like a huge draught horse, Balzac
> yawns, snorts, lumbers
> to the watercloset
> and, flinging open his gown,
> trains a great stream of piss into the
> early nineteenth century
> chamberpot. The lace curtain catches
> the breeze. Wait! One last scene
> before sleep. His brain sizzles as
> he goes back to his desk – the pen,
> the pot of ink, the strewn pages.[3]

A Painter of our Time is not a journal; it is a novel. This has provided critics with a convenient excuse for neglecting it as fiction and refusing to consider its ideas. Berger might have talent as an art critic, the argument runs, but a novel is not written by an art critic; novels are written by novelists. Only a Marxist reviewer like Arnold Kettle in *Labour Monthly* could declare himself 'not much interested' in whether or not *A Painter of our Time* was 'technically perfect' as a novel. Elsewhere the response was both virulent and dismissive. (When these two reactions are combined you have a sure sign of the perplexed critic.) For Stephen Spender in the

Observer (9 November 1958), Lavin was 'an advocate of judicial murder' and his notebooks were comparable with Goebbels' *Michael*. The journal *Encounter* (which at the time was CIA backed) ran a violently hostile review, and within a few months Secker and Warburg – who published both *Encounter* and *A Painter of our Time* – withdrew the book.

The violence of the attack on Lavin's journal, however, goes some way to cancelling out the objections to Berger as a writer of fiction – appeals to the autonomy of fiction simultaneously deny it; aesthetic imperatives lead to a refusal to consider the book's aesthetic merits. But the vehement objections to Lavin are tributes to Berger's power of fictional creation, an affirmation of the independent life with which Lavin has been endowed. There is little sign *within* the novel that the ageing Lavin is the 'creation' of a 30-year-old writer: his voice is an authentic product of the events he has lived through.

His political and artistic views are obviously close to Berger's:

Yet still we must recognize that *any* extension of the range of human imagination is a contribution to our aim. . . I believe we have made a profound mistake whenever we have used our marxism to make an arbitrary division between art that is for us (progressive art) and art which is against us (decadent art). All good art is for Man – and therefore for us. . . My contribution has been very small, but it is dangerous to try to make it bigger. Do not demand Socialist Art. (*P.T.* pp. 146-7)

There is clearly a lot of Berger in Lavin but, since the other principal character in the book – John, the young socialist art critic – resembles Berger so markedly, it is he who appears to be the author's representative in the novel. It does not matter then that Lavin's views are similar to Berger's; the important thing – within the logic of the novel – is that Lavin's and John's voices do not 'merge'. This distance between John and Lavin is absolutely central to the book.

Janos Lavin is a Hungarian emigré and communist. He begins painting in his early 20s in Prague, having left Hungary after the overthrow of the revolutionary Soviet government of 1919. In 1938 he is forced to flee again, this time to England, from the Nazis. In England he married a young English woman, Diana, and they live in his small studio. She works as a librarian; Janos earns a little money teaching at the local art school. Despite the efforts of John, Lavin receives little recognition in England but in 1956 he holds a successful exhibition and sells several paintings. It is just after this exhibition that Lavin disappears. A letter reveals that he has gone to Budapest in the midst of the Hungarian uprising but what he has done there is unclear.

In his youth, Lavin had been an abstract constructivist. The paintings he produces in Britain are opposed both to narrow social realism and the growing taste for abstraction. His paintings are large and bright, reminiscent of Leger. While working on the canvas called *The Swimmer* Lavin goes out for the day and the impressions he records in his journal evoke the spirit of his own canvases and those of Leger:

> People were streaming out of London, dressed in brightly
> coloured cottons and silks – charabancs, motorbikes, bicycles,
> tandems, cars, lorries full of children. Everywhere you looked
> people were lying on the green grass; some in each others arms;
> some with newspapers over their faces. It was like seeing a
> straight play that the sun had suddenly turned into a comedy.
> (*P.T.* p.57)

A curious and significant effect of the novel, however, is the insistent sense that Lavin is not a great painter. When we begin reading we tend automatically to assume that Lavin's journal is to be the diary of a genius but it soon becomes apparent that the book emphatically takes its standards from what is common rather than exceptional, from what is shared rather than what is exclusive, from what is essential rather than outstanding. Painter and barber share a common aim:

> Every so often [the barber] stepped back to squint at my hair,
> his head on one side, his eyes screwed up. The gesture was
> exactly the same as a painter's when he looks at his canvas. He
> wanted to see what he had done freshly, he wanted to see it in
> the best possible and most flattering light, but he also wanted to
> see it truthfully. That's the conflict of aim that makes us squint.
> But it is a gesture not only confined to barbers and painters. It is
> the worldwide gesture of men measuring their original work.
> (*P.T.* p.53)

In describing the socialist victory that he works for, Lavin might well have added these lines from an article of Berger's in the *New*

Statesman: 'There will be no such victory until reasonable talent, as opposed to genius, can produce satisfying works of art.'

But Berger is reluctant to relinquish the notion of genius and so he has Lavin define it in terms of a huge capacity for empathy:

> Genius is never a case apart. It is utterly opposed to mania. The genius bears the full weight of what is common, of what exists hundreds and thousands of times over. But he watches himself and that is what separates him from others. (*P.T.* p.65)

Not surprisingly Lavin's thought is close to what Berger felt was the genius of Leger:

> Leger was only concerned with what we have in common. . . Leger's vision of the genius was of a man with an imagination so in tune with his time, and therefore so easily understandable, that he could become almost anonymous. (*P.R.* p.125)

By defining it in these terms, the concept of genius is forcibly democratized at the expense of its usefulness as a distinguishing term. To observe closely is to discriminate; the word genius is a mark of distinction. Berger's own need to distinguish genius from talent testifies to the semantic urge towards the exceptional – away from the common ground – of the notion of genius. Even if we use the word to denote or describe a particular way or kind of working then we are drawn back to an implicit value judgement since the chief characteristic of the genius is that he or she produces works which are shockingly better than they have any right to be. The genius is always surprising. He or she frequently lacks any ability to estimate his/her own work critically. Typically, the genius leaves few clues as to how he or she produces the work in question.

By contrast, Lavin's work, we get the impression, seems exactly as good as it ought to be. The genius on the other hand – like Picasso – is unpredictable; Lavin and Picasso seem directly opposed in Berger's imagination. Lavin speaks of the duty we owe to our talents; Picasso, says Berger, accords more value to his own creativity than to what he creates. Lavin strives and searches; Picasso discovers effortlessly. 'Painting is stronger than I am. It makes me do what it wants', says Picasso; Lavin would say in reply that 'history is stronger than painters, they should do what history requires of them'. Picasso is a voluntary exile, Lavin is a refugee. Berger defines both their lives in terms of success and failure:

Lavin is a measure of Picasso's failure; Picasso is the measure of Lavin's.

The limitations of Lavin's work – his failure – are products of the limitations imposed on him by his circumstances. 'Success,' wrote Berger in the same year that *A Painter of our Time* was published, 'meaning appreciative understanding by a large number of people, is essential.'[5] 'For the artist, inventing, satisfying, defying his public is an integral part of the act of creation', writes Tim Clark; 'It is when one of those stances towards the public becomes an autonomous or over-riding consideration . . . or when the public becomes either too abstract and unreal a concept, that a radical sickness of art begins.'[6] Lavin's art is sick – in the sense of ailing – precisely because of this situation. The condition of exile is not simply one of geographical or national displacement. As Lavin says,

> In one way or another [the painter in Budapest] is fighting for his place among his fellow men; he is fighting about the terms on which his contribution is not just wanted but demanded. I have no choice but to paint as I must. But I would like to be a useful man again. (*P.T.* p.118)

Talk, Lavin observes on another occasion, 'soon makes nonsense of monologues'; robbed of a dialogue with his public, Lavin's art suffers from the limitations of monologue. Lavin's style, as George Steiner said of Lukács, 'is that of the exile; it has lost the habits of living speech.'[7] The piece of paper with MAY I OFFER YOU MY HEARTFELT CONGRATULATIONS on it was, it turns out, given to Lavin by a colleague from the art school who was dumb. Lavin was moved by the gesture and kept the paper because he too is, in a sense, dumb: 'gagged by the silence of others'.[8]

At the time of writing the novel, Berger knew many artists like Lavin, but the fictional character is based principally on two Hungarian emigrés whom Berger knew personally: Frederick Antal and Peter Peri.

Berger met Peri, a painter and sculptor, in 1952; he visited his studio, they attended political meetings together and discussed the project of the novel at length. Peri was enthusiastic about the idea but Berger never found out what he thought of the completed novel. 'He probably thought it inadequate. Even if he had thought otherwise, I think it would have been impossible for him to tell me. By that time the habit of suffering inaccessibility, like the habit of eating meagre vegetable soup, had become too strong."[9]

Lavin shares some of Peri's personal characteristics and many of the qualities Berger admired in Peri's work are ascribed to Lavin's. Peri's works are 'vibrant with the idea of humanity . . . at their best they express what he believed in.' Anthony Blunt's comments on Peri, from an introduction to the catalogue for a 1970 exhibition, throws light on Lavin:

> He had been through the hard training of constructivism; he was aware of all the most advanced schools had to offer; but he was determined to create an art which should not appeal only to a limited and intellectually snobbish group.
>
> It was a surprise to him, and a disappointment to his friends, that the importance of his work was not immediately recognized. . . In due course . . . he was occasionally given the opportunity of doing what he thought was really worthwhile, but to the end he suffered from a feeling of frustration.[10]

Lavin is by no means simply a portrait of Peri. The title and sub-title of the novel, 'A Portrait of the Artist as Emigré', (recalling Joyce and Lermontov respectively) stress that Lavin is the representative of a general condition of artists. Lavin's sense of a duty owed to one's capabilities recalls Berger's observation on Josef Herman – that even his weaker works are marked by 'the rare discipline that is the result of an artist knowing that he serves something larger than his own talent.'[11] (Berger also applies to Herman the line of Gorki's that forms the epigraph to *A Painter*: 'The world will always be bad enough for the desire for something better not to be extinguished in men.') In the novel, Hardwick, the principal of the art school, explains, 'Mr Lavin is our link with tradition.' And so he is – but not in the way Hardwick had in mind. He is the link with the tradition of scholar-activists for whom communism is 'the root-fibre of [their] intelligence'[12], men and women for whom 'the only meaning of life is conscious participation in the making of history.'[13]

Lavin's exile represents the last historic condition of that tradition, a condition of defeat but not of surrender. Vague notions of the artist in exile have become a cliché; *A Painter* grounds its idea of exile in a specific history. Lavin lives by historical necessity and holds himself responsible to history. 'The greatest violinist', he writes, 'cannot be justified in playing his violin on the bank of a river in which a drowning man is shouting for help.' In leaving for Hungary he follows the dictates of history, not so much abandoning art for activism as living by the logic of the revolutionary rather than the exile. His situation dramatizes not simply the crisis of an individual conscience at a particular moment but the transition between two *conditions* (epoch is too strong a word) of history.

Peter Fuller has also noticed the larger historical scheme of the novel: 'If, in the novel, Hungary represents History to which Lavin is always struggling to relate his work, Sir Gerald Banks, the man who buys several of Lavin's paintings represents the apparently benign bourgeoisie, always endeavouring to obstruct the process by assimilation of the artist and his works'. Similarly, the London fog corresponds to 'Britain's insular bourgeois ideology'.[14] While there may be truth in these comments, these terms are too schematic, giving little sense of how the novel contains, dramatically, its own historical purpose. There is no need to go to these allegorical lengths.

Reading *A Painter of our Time* today, we are struck by how remote is the world depicted. The reason for this is, I think, that the book is deeply nostalgic. In a key passage of the book Lavin thinks of his old friend Laszlo:

> When he walked away from you his jacket hung from his shoulders and his trousers from his hips as though they were never taken off, like clothes hanging for months in the Jewish secondhand shops that were being smashed up. By then he wore spectacles. He belonged to that unique fraternity of scholars, the activist scholars of marxism. In every photograph from 1910 onwards you find their faces. I know that beside them I look like a nineteenth-century romantic. They are shortsighted from reading and they are often frail in physique. But they have known they can change the world. (*P.T.* p.102)

This is, above all, a nostalgic image. It is to that 'unique fraternity' and time that Lavin and Berger hark back.

The year 1956 stands as the moment of symbolic divide between two historic conditions of the revolutionary left in Britain. (That the two conditions are not as suddenly divisible as such a claim implies does not matter – it is the symbolic content of the year that does.) Lavin leaves for Budapest in the midst of this crisis: but it is by no means certain what he does when he arrives.

> Did he stand by and watch those terrible days in Budapest? Did he join with the revisionists of the Petöfi circle? Did he fight side by side with those workers' councils who resisted the Red Army? Did he oppose this resistance and was he lynched by a mob as a Rakosi agent? Is he now a supporter of the Kadar government or does he bide his time? Each of these possibilities is reasonable. And the full tragedy of the Hungarian situation is revealed by the fact that we, who have the advantage of knowing some of this man's most intimate hopes, thoughts, confessions, cannot with any certainty declare which of these courses of action he was bound to follow. (*P.T.* p.190)

The novel ends in the midst of this confused moment of historical divide.

This is the importance of John's parallel commentary. It is written from the other side of that symbolic divide and looks back nostalgically across it. While Lavin has no place in post-1956 England, is isolated and can only practice what he feels has become 'a very limited art', John moves effortlessly between dealers, exhibition organizers, students, and socialist artists. Although he might despise them, he is part of exactly the same phase of historical development as the gallery owners and dealers. He is dependent on the same material transformations in the relation of art to society: rising prices, increasing interest in art, more need of critics and guides to mediate between the artist and the public. He has his place in what will become the New Left but the active option that existed for Lavin, the classic revolutionary tradition that formed him, is no longer available to John. Lavin's political commitment has been tested and hardened in the fire of history. John is part of the post-war settlement, a socialist intellectual whose radicalism is safe from the cutting edge of history. Unlike Jimmy Porter, he knows that there are good, brave causes left to fight for but he does his fighting comfortably, as an art critic. Lavin tells John that it is difficult for him 'to imagine what it meant to be a revolutionary'. John concludes that Lavin 'thought that it was impossible to hope that any of his intimates could understand the crisis he was facing'. John's reflection on Diana applies also to himself:

She had never been hungry. She had never been interrogated. She had never been smuggled over a frontier. She had sat in committee rooms. She had shouted in Trafalgar Square. . . But the way she had arrived at doing such things always remained there as a possible way of retreat. She had never been cut off. Whereas Janos was entirely cut off. (*P.T.* p.24)

John's distance from Lavin is paralleled by Berger's distance from Peter Peri:

He considered that our experience was inadequate. We had not been in Budapest at the time of the Soviet Revolution. We had not seen how Bela Kun had been, perhaps unnecessarily, defeated. We had not been in Berlin in 1920. We did not know how the possibility of a revolution in Germany had been betrayed. We had not witnessed the creeping advance and then the terrifying triumph of Nazism.[16] (*L.T.* p.63)

The year 1956 was the symbolic moment when political choices stopped being simple. Before that choices were hard *because* the options were simple. Since then, as Berger wrote in the preface to the new edition of *Permanent Red*:

The future perspective of the world has changed fundamentally. In the early 1950s . . . there were two poles, and only two, to which any political thought and action inevitably led. The polarization was between Moscow and Washington. Only when the USSR achieved (or was reckoned to have achieved) parity in nuclear arms with the USA could this struggle cease to be the primary political factor. The achieving of this parity just preceded the Twentieth Congress of the CPSU and the Polish and Hungarian uprisings, to be followed later by the first obvious divergences between the USSR and China and by the victory of the Cuban Revolution. Revolutionary examples and possibilities have since multiplied. The raison d'etre of polarized dogmatism has collapsed. (*P.R.* pp.7-8)

Lavin disappears into the midst of the moment of transition. Immediately after that moment, in the new condition of history, the seeds of the revolutionary impetus of May 1968 can be found.

4. *The Foot of Clive* and *Corker's Freedom*

The Foot of Clive is a bad novel that should be a play; even then it would not be a very good one but on screen or stage its inadequacies could generate a certain momentum; on the page they simply draw attention to themselves.

Named after Clive of India, Clive is a hospital ward where six men are waiting for or recovering from surgery. Dai, 67, a casual labourer and crude bully is in hospital for a growth under his arm. Ken is an advertising executive, in hospital after a road accident involving a motorcyclist. Harry, in his late forties, is a fitter; good-natured and tolerant, he is distinguished from the others by 'his attempt to live in Clive actively rather than passively. He treats Clive as another job'. Robin is a schoolboy from a fairly privileged background, in hospital for a badly-injured knee. Cyril is the oldest and illest; when conscious he is prone to bursts of evangelical fervour. Set slightly apart from the rest is Pepino, an Italian who has lost a hand in an air disaster; he is worried about his wife Renata who is giving birth to their child back in Italy. In the dim background are other characters like the man who appears to have known all temptations, referred to throughout, with prescient allegorical shorthand, as the temptation man.

Berger's intentions in a novel set in a hospital might be expected to resemble those of Trevor Griffiths, who described his TV play *All Through the Night* as 'a demand for the audience to see the hospital as a site of so much more than romance between doctors and nurses . . . to ask questions about hospitalization, the National Health Service, the relationships between experts and non-experts.'[1] Not a bit of it. The novel's plot revolves around the arrival in the ward of Jack House, a murderer who was badly injured when arrested. As word gets around the ward the other characters are thrown into shock and then galvanized into action; outrage gives way to violent confrontation. At the same time, Pepino tries to escape and the police arrive to question Ken about his accident: under interrogation it turns out that Ken and the motorcyclist had been racing each other along a stretch of road; the cyclist has since died of his injuries. The deadpan naturalism of the opening scenes gives way to some lengthy and feverish interior monologues – like this one from Ken:

Case of Motor Cyclist's Death. Tried. Yes Sir. Death through misadventure. That is to say, mistake, through consequences of misspent life. Always lied. Lied to mother. Believe my own lies. Gone that far. Stole too. In handbag with photo of me and father. Too stupid to notice. Push on. Bash on. Fuck you. On and on. (*F.C.* p.87)

On and on, exactly – though it is not till Part 3, 'The Execution', that things get really out of hand. In a long hallucinatory sequence the sleeping characters merge into each other's dreams. Prose gives way to dramatic notation; Berger cries 'havoc' and lets slip the dogs of Clive. The dogs are at the thematic and dramatic core of the book. The narrative of the first section is broken up by pronouncements about dogs in familiar Berger style:

Dogs wait beside their masters like servants who have not been given their instructions. . . It is the faithfulness of the dog that makes it possible for people to talk about his being treacherous. (*F.C.* p.28)

No other animal except the human baby seems to be capable of sustaining its complaint for so long as the dog. . . Its purpose [the dog's howling], like the cries of the human baby, but unlike the call of any other animal, is to attract man. And such is the dog's inherited faith in man that often he will cry all night. (*F.C.* p.32)

No dog is of any use as a witness. His eyes can see, his nose can recognize, his tongue can confirm, but he can make no statement. He has neither language nor concepts. The truth for him is only the scent on the wind. (*F.C.* p.40)

On occasions dogs behave like the wolves or jackals from which they are anciently descended. (*F.C.* p.36)

These chunks of dog lore are woven into the naturalist text through puns ('Being a messenger must be a dog's life'; 'he's not like some of the patients who go around like dying dogs') and remembered events in the characters' lives.

Sinister connections between past events and the patients' current illnesses are suggested by Robin, Ken and Dai. Robin, in hospital for a knee operation, thinks of how his dog had broken a leg after falling 'out of the window which they said he, Robin, had left open'. Remembering the dalmatian that used always to accompany his lover, Eleanor, Ken recalls how 'he'd once thought of running that dog down'. Half-asleep, Dai dreams that he is 'chasing, bounding, leaping, following his pug nose'. Then dream gives way to the more vivid memory of an actual chase in his childhood. Dai and some friends had succeeded in trapping and killing a deer. Matt, the ringleader, gutted the animal and from its stomach 'drew out some leaves, still green, and two apples whole and untouched. The animal's swallowing of these apples had polished them. Their russet skins were shiny.' Matt offers a shilling to anyone who will dare to eat one of them. Dai snatches one of the apples and eats it, core and all. The growth under his arm is, we have already been told, 'hard and large as an apple'.

In the surreal swirl of Part 3 'the dogs, who once only dared to enter dreams, have been emboldened by the last day's events'. They can now be heard in Clive when everyone is awake. 'Each man knows a dog is near, and this knowledge transforms his surroundings.' The dogs seem to represent the spirit of night, darkness, death but the dramatics that give expression to the idea are difficult to take seriously. The characters drive themselves towards a screeching apotheosis. They rave and howl in rabid outpourings. Clive is like Bedlam; everyone is shouting all sorts of rubbish. Cyril, for instance, manages to whip himself up into a frenzy of religious fervour; In his demented ecstasy Cyril confesses that he raped his wife 'to save her soul' (disagreeable memories of Telly Savalas in *The Dirty Dozen* come back here as Cyril lapses into evangelical rapist mode). By this time Clive is 'full of the noises of Golgotha'; in what seems a parody of the occasional excesses of Theatre of the Absurd everyone continues to shout about the dogs: 'The dogs!'; 'Can you hear the dogs?'

Ken: There's a dog barking.
Dai: Always those damned dogs. Who would think they
  -   need dogs in Clive?
Ken: There is a dog for each of us.
Robin: I wish I could get comfortable.
Dai: The best way is to talk – to talk it out.

'It's the dogs that get me,' says Dai on another occasion, speaking for us all. 'Can't you keep quiet about the dogs?' snaps back Ken in an even more precise echo of the reader's sentiments.

After his confession, Cyril dies; four dogs stand at each corner of his bed. The rest of the ward imagines 'the dogs inside Cyril's town . . . prowl[ing] through the ruins, pawing all to dust'. Next morning the four survivors wait, like 'the four dogs at the four corners of Cyril's bed', like 'the four other watchers, the four soldiers who guarded the tomb of Christ on the night of the Resurrection'. Simultaneously, Pepino, who, as a result of a massive injection, had been 'free of the dogs', cries out 'Maria!' and announces the birth of a son.

The two final sections return to naturalistic conventions and the characters reflect on what has happened to them; in some way they feel vaguely that they have been tested and chastened by their experience in Clive. The last we hear of the dogs is from Dai: 'I'll have a dog to keep me company in the shop', he says.

At first, Clive is seen as a sealed, self-enclosed world: 'The windows of Clive are inked over. . . The only tokens now of the outside world are the words that come over the radio.' (These words, with news of House, the murderer, presage the invasion of Clive by House himself a little later.) The ward is seen as the collective embodiment of different lives in a way that is strongly reminiscent of Tom-All-Alones in *Bleak House* – 'Clive is agitated, palms wet. Clive is living to have its say' – but without any of the emotional force or urgency of the Dickens creation. In spite of Berger's modernist aside that at visiting time, Clive becomes 'a city of words', a text indistinguishable from the fictional world of the novel as a whole, Clive remains what it is all the time striving to be more than – an arena of individual confrontations. With this in mind, it is difficult to share Berger's claim that 'there is much to be learnt in Clive for those with eyes to see and ears to hear'.

That Clive is intended as a microcosm of the larger world outside is suggested by a passage near the end of the novel, when Robin looks out of a window and sees the world of Clive writ large: 'He saw an iron fire escape like the one Pepino had made his way down. He saw an aeroplane in the sky like the one that had crashed. He saw the newsagent's and it was like Cyril's shop. . . In the car park was a sports car like Ken's. He saw the lives lived behind the dark walls.' (*F.C.* p.155) He goes on to infer that the characters in Clive stand for those in the larger world and translates them into representatives of the animal kingdom:

He saw Ken and Harry and Dai. Their names were now like ordinary nouns to him. He could define them. Kens were timid. Nobody could get very near them. They went fast. They hid well . . . Kens were bucks . . . Harrys were elephants. Dais lived on their wits. They went their own way. They were seldom at a loss unless they were cornered. . . Dais were rats and he liked them above all. (*F.C.* pp. 155-6)

Typical or average? Typical only insofar as the characters gathered together on an airliner, ship or skyscraper in a disaster movie are typical. The animal allegories complete the formal scheme of the book without enlarging on its significance. We remain slightly dazed, unsure of what has happened and still faintly numb as if coming round from an anaesthetic. Although the dialogue has an authentic ring to it, Berger's realist ambitions are spoilt by laboured anthropomorphism and insistent allegories (Cyril as Christ). Elsewhere the combination of naturalist dialogue and absurdist ravings put one more in mind of the tinkerings of N. F. Simpson than the exacting interrogations of Pinter. 'What is the absurd?' Berger is to write in *G*. 'Only a moment of incongruity between two different systems of thinking.' That moment has produced some of the century's masterpieces. The *sustained* incongruity of different elements in *The Foot of Clive* makes for silliness rather than absurdity, obfuscation rather than illumination. There is an uneasy marriage between the Olympian tone of Berger's pronouncements and the seediness of what he is pronouncing upon. What would develop into the 'secularized, millenial tone' of *G* is unnecessarily grand in the earlier novel: 'By their nature, all allotments are small.' 'The whisper is not for the sake of propriety; it is to intensify meaning.' Berger tries too hard to intensify his meaning in these matchbox dictats.

There are good things in *The Foot of Clive*: the smell of the hospital, 'like a mixture of lemons and sour milk'; brief glimpses of the city outside Clive waking up and going to work: 'In the city beyond Clive, the streets, trains and buses are crowded with people hurrying home. Most of them buy an evening paper. These papers are thus distributed throughout the entire city. The news falls everywhere like snow.' (*F.C.* p. 17) Some scenes are powerfully done but it is indicative of the overall failure of the book that the best touches are incidental rather than central to the main action.

✳

Corker's Freedom is no more satisfactory. *The Foot of Clive* proceeds energetically enough; *Corker's Freedom* lurches forward a second at a time like an electric clock at a station. Each sentence is tensed in a portentous and mildly ironic present, offering itself to the reader like an index card in a filing drawer. If the intention is to mimic the tedium of office routine then Berger has succeeded for we respond in kind – flicking through instead of reading. Dialogue, interior monologues and various asides merge together in interminable, stifling paragraphs.

The novel covers one momentous day in the life of Corker who runs what the blurb of the latest edition, in an attempt to give the novel some contemporaneity, inaccurately calls an unemployment agency in Clapham. Corker's is an employment agency; the novel is set in 1960 when dole offices were called Labour Exchanges and there was work to go round. Almost everybody on Corker's books gets offered work in a day or two. A selection of punters come into the office and are attended to by Corker and his assistant Alec. Alec is 17, has just slept with his girlfriend for the first time, and keeps his own mental file of the day's events. The first 50 or so pages are concerned with the inflexible routine of the office – filling out cards, filing mail, phoning prospective employers – and with Corker's treatment of his customers. The customers themselves are depicted with a deadpan accuracy that has something of the patronising effect of superior politeness. What is really a prejudiced selection of detail tries to pass itself off as an objective rendering of reality. The resulting tone is condescending rather than ironic. Irony depends on discretion; condescension is indiscreet and is the natural handmaiden of naturalism. What surprises us most about *Corker's Freedom* is its pervasive naturalism. Those who come to Corker's office are observed with no more sensitivity than in an English comedy film of the same era.

> Seven pounds, she says, phew it's hot in here, do you mind if I take my coat off? She takes off the black overcoat with the fur collar. Underneath she is wearing a short-sleeved green blouse, the colour of willow leaves. Her arms are plump and white except for the backs of her forearms which are freckled.
> (*C.F.* p.27)

Here is the method of naturalism in precision miniature: each individual detail of observation reinforces not the individual but the stereotype. The simple distinction between realism and naturalism is that naturalism works always at the expense of the individual; details are accumulated in order to fill out the mould of the average.

In his criticism, Berger had insisted that realism was not simply a technique but an attitude of mind. The naturalism of *Corker's Freedom*, however, stems from an uncertain technique. Sometimes the observations of customers mirror Corker's own index of classification or Alec's lusty appraisal. Thus it is Corker who notes Mrs McBryde's 'full round breasts' and Alec who notes that Miss Marlow's breasts are a 'nice size'. But it is Berger who makes the same Miss Marlow think of Wednesday afternoon as 'the only weekday time which is hers to dispense with dusky promise to those whose longing to see her again is worthy of sweet encouragement'. If Alec undresses Miss Marlow with his eyes Berger intrudes into her consciousness, clothing her with the mocking voice of implicit value judgements.

Miss Marlow arrives when Corker's extraordinary day is already well under way. That morning Corker had walked out on Irene, the invalid sister with whom he had lived for 12 years. She rings throughout the day, making veiled threats and disturbing Corker, whose thoughts and uncertainties interrupt more and more frequently the description of office routine. By the time Yvonne Browning enters the office the text is fairly evenly divided between what is happening and what Corker is thinking. Yvonne is there to case the office for a housebreaker named Wolff who is planning to do it over. He gets his chance earlier than expected since Corker is so impressed by Yvonne's genteel manners that he invites her to a talk on Vienna that he is giving that evening.

Before that, in the afternoon, Corker gets Alec to help him rearrange the rooms above the office so that he can move in there now that he has left his sister. In the intimacy of shared exertion, Corker tells Alec that when he played as a child, he, Corker, 'used to be Sir Lancelot'; for the rest of the afternoon he drifts off intermittently into this sub-Joycean parallel life. In the course of the furniture moving, Corker cuts his finger and waits for Alec to fetch the iodine:

Corker makes believe: And behold Sir Lancelot saw a vision. His young squire mounted on a fair horse, well saddled and bridled, rode into the clearing of wood wherein Sir Lancelot lay bleeding with none to do dole for him. And the squire full young and tender of age dismounted Sir Lancelot. (*C.F.* p. 109)

In the evening Corker arrives drunk at the vicarage to give his talk. Yvonne Browning comes to the talk to make sure Corker does not go back early and surprise Wolff who is burgling the office. Corker's talk is illustrated with slides that are flashed onto the printed page in bold type, A STATUE OF SCHILLER; THE IMPERIAL GARDENS AT DUSK, and for 80 long pages we listen to a combination of Corker's yearning thoughts and his increasingly drunken lecture. The vicar, already alarmed by some of Corker's lewd jokes, interrupts the lecture when Corker recalls that as he was passing a horse, 'a natural function had just begun'. After a break for tea the lecture begins again and Corker wobbles off on wilder and wilder tangents: 'What is the hurry?' he wonders, 'does it seem that efficiency is the most important thing in life? Or duty either? Why must we always put off what we want? Why do we all postpone happiness?' The lecture ends in some confusion. Irene (who has arrived in the middle of the talk) leaves and Yvonne chases out after her to prevent her going to the office. In a scuffle, Irene falls to the pavement and Corker returns to the office to find that he has been burgled.

A postscript explains what has happened to the characters: Irene died; Wolff and Yvonne were arrested. Because the drunken Corker had forgotten to lock the office door he was assumed to be in league with the criminals and so he is unable to claim insurance. Ruined, Corker is last seen as a tipsy speaker at Hyde Park corner.

Writing in *The Look of Things*, Berger observes of Rousseau that all he inherited 'was the usual stale deposit of petit bourgeois clichés. His imagination, his imaginative experience was always in conflict with his received culture'. Because 'such conflicts have not yet been properly understood or described' he chose them as the theme for *Corker's Freedom*.[2] In *A Fortunate Man*, Berger notes that *Corker's Freedom* is an attempt to illuminate the situation of those who 'are deprived of the means of translating what they know into thoughts which they can think.'[3] Trapped by his aspirations, the most Corker can do is, as Irene savagely reflects, 'sniff at the fine horse's dung like a dog'.

The book itself cannot support such weighty ambitions (though there are moments of genuine pathos – as when Corker considers that 'it is not I who have wasted my gifts and it is not I who have suffered as a result, it is my gifts themselves that have remained discontented and it is life that has wasted them'). Corker's comparisons of himself with Sir Lancelot, his inebriated rhetoric and his yearning aspirations are not adequately transformed or distinguished from the petit bourgeois clichés in which they are expressed. The novel is 'stuck' at the first parodic level, as unable, despite the pervasive influence of Joyce, to rise to its ambitions as Corker himself.

Berger's subsequent explanation of his intentions should not divert us from seeing that what he says of Corker could as easily and accurately be applied to the character of whom he insistently reminds me: Captain Mainwaring in the TV series *Dad's Army*. Mainwaring fits Berger's scheme surprisingly neatly. Like Corker, Mainwaring is frequently compared, by the ARP warden, with a historical-mythical antecedent: Napoleon. Further, although he is a bank manager and captain in the Home Guard, the cultural and military ambitions of this ex-grammar school boy are constantly sabotaged by the class antagonism that exists between him and the languid, aristocratic, public school educated Sergeant Wilson.

Dad's Army is also, of course, a good deal funnier than Berger's novel. *Corker's Freedom* is the only one of Berger's books with any light-hearted intention but the oddly stilted diction and the characteristic deliberateness of his prose work against humour. Even Corker's drunken Vienna lecture is surprisingly unfunny given the circumstances; you see that it's not meant to be entirely serious but it never actually makes you laugh. David Gervais has noted that in Berger's fiction 'the idea always precludes the imaginative rendering of it' and that is why, he says, Corker is lifeless.[4]

We will return to this idea in the conclusion; for the moment, though, this chapter must end on a note of some puzzlement. Berger's career has been marked by abrupt changes of style and ambition, but the massive qualitative rupture between his first novel, a masterpiece, and the two subsequent ones is baffling. Appropriately, his next book is concerned with issues of success and failure; in it he returns to art criticism but, as he commented later, it is art criticism written 'somewhat like a novel'.

5. Picasso and Cubism

Marxist analysis of art tends to situate rather than explain.[1] The socioeconomic situation in which the artist finds him or herself determines, in Raymond Williams's sense of *setting limits* and exerting pressure, rather than *causing*. However, an understanding of *situation* does not explain why Picasso, rather than someone in similar circumstances, became the greatest artist of the twentieth century. 'Valéry is a petit bourgeois intellectual, no doubt about it. But not every petit bourgeois intellectual is Valéry', said Sartre, providing the epigraph to all subsequent discussion of subjective agency versus historical determinism.[2] To explain why it was Valéry and not some other person we need as much information as possible on his mental and physical biography; but since the amount of available information will always be inadequate, the nature of the creative act is bound to remain more or less elusive. Picasso's artistic methods can be explained in terms of his precocious talent as a child, but we are unlikely ever to know why he was able to draw so well so young. To know *exactly* why certain artists developed in a certain way at a certain time, writes Berger in 'The Moment of Cubism', 'we would need to know an impossible amount about each separate development. In that impossibility – which is an absolute one – lies our freedom from determinism.'[3]

The Success and Failure of Picasso is the first of two full-length studies that Berger devoted to an individual artist. It is his most sustained piece of practical criticism. From an early self-portrait in which 'we see the face of a man who not only is cold and hasn't eaten much, but who is also silent and to whom nobody speaks', to *Guernica* – 'Picasso appeals to nothing more elevated than our instinct for survival' – the observations and analyses of the paintings he admires are striking, original and persuasive. The larger aim of the book, though, is to combine a detailed reconstruction of relevant Spanish history with both an account of Picasso's formal development and a speculative, intuitive and informed attempt to understand the way in which Picasso's temperament responded to and was formed by these circumstances.*

'Art is an interplay, an equation of three factors – the artist, the world and the means of configuration,' wrote Max Raphael, and in attempting to define Picasso in relation to these three coordinates, Berger's debt to Raphael, 'a forgotten but great critic', is obvious.[4] Raphael's essay on Picasso in *Proudhon, Marx, Picasso* (first published in German in 1933) provides Berger with the theoretical framework for his own study. Like Berger, Raphael locates Picasso at the confluence of historical forces; unlike Berger's, Raphael's analysis of these forces is often difficult and dense. Picasso's youth, says Raphael, coincided with the period when 'free enterprise was being supplanted by monopoly capitalism. The general character of this transition and the special conditions in which it was effected in Spain exerted a crucial, though in part unconscious influence on the painter.'[5] The peculiarities of Spain's historical development meant that what for other European countries had been distinct phases of the historical process occurred simultaneously in Spain. At the same time that the transition from free enterprise to monopoly capitalism was taking place, the Spanish bourgeoisie was still engaged in 'heroic battles against feudalism and the church'. This time of violent conflict between the old and the new, 'of powerful, violent tensions', was marked by three distinctive features: 'increase in vitality, polarization of contradictions, and the need for comprehensible norms'.[6] These features, the characteristics of 'all truly crucial epochs', find their

---

* At the same time that Berger tries to relate all the facts that can be publicly known about Picasso, his book is highly selective rather than rigorously comprehensive. About a third of *Picasso* is concerned with the Cubist years from 1907 to 1914. Berger discusses virtually none of the works produced after 1953, and deals fairly briefly with those after 1945, and in what he later admitted was his impatience to get to the Cubist years he 'failed to see . . . the importance of a number of works from about 1902 to about 1907' (*New Society* 8 October 1981 p.68). Berger's economy of method is a consistent strength, but selectivity may also distort. In the book, Berger considers that none of Picasso's work since 1945 shows 'any advance on what he created before' – an opinion with which we may agree or disagree but since one of Berger's theses is that Picasso was unable to find subjects, he prejudices his case unfairly by giving the impression that with the exception of a few parodies of Velasquez and the Clown, Artist, Monkey, Nude series of drawings (1953) Picasso produced virtually nothing after that year.

way into Picasso's art. Picasso's artistic development is explained in these terms:

> Just as in monopoly capitalism, there is a widening gap between private property and planned economic organization, so that economic and social crises grow ever more acute, so in Picasso the dualism between his fundamental individualism and his mathematical, generalized means of expression lead to ever more pronounced psychic crises. This accounts for the continual modification in his 'style', the different forms of which all revolve around the same unsolved problems.[7]

Berger draws very obviously on Raphael's analysis to develop his own model of Spain as a country stretched on an historical rack. This 'rack', says Berger, has not bred 'those contradictions which can lead to further development: instead there is unchanging poverty and a terrible equilibrium.' Hence, in Spain, the attraction of anarchism which ignores all process of development and offers instead a sudden, violent reversal of the social order.

Unlike Raphael, Berger does not draw precise correspondences between the historical development of Spain and Picasso's art. The connection is made by two resonant quotations – one from Bakunin and one from Picasso. 'Let us put our trust in the eternal spirit which destroys and annihilates only because it is the unsearchable and eternally creative source of all life. The urge to destroy is also a creative urge,' (S.F.P. p.22) says Bakunin. 'A painting', says Picasso, 'is a sum of destructions.'

Berger has a knack for bringing quotations into suggestive proximity. Like all great essayists he suggests connections without labouring them. At various points in the book he 'quotes' or juxtaposes images without comment: Picasso's *Head of a Horse* of 1937 and Rubens' *Christ Crucified* of 1620; Picasso's *Portrait of Mrs. H.P.* of 1952 and Van Gogh's *Portrait of the Superintendent of the Saint Remy Asylum* of 1889. The reader is left to make connections, to see similarities, to provide the answer to a question Berger has asked and, thus, to complete Berger's argument for him.

The terms of Picasso's creative personality are established in a similar way. Berger does not look straight at Picasso – staring at an enigma only enhances its enigmative elusiveness. Instead he looks to others, to Picasso's left and right, as it were, in order to see Picasso at illuminating, refracted angles of insight. Picasso is 'bounced off' a number of mirrors. At odd moments in his eclectic reading, one gets the impression, Berger would come across a passage which, *suitably tilted*, would give an oddly-angled reflection of Picasso. There is, perhaps, something reminiscent of the Cubist method about this. Thus Picasso is inspired neither by muse nor angel, but by the fiery and dangerous spirit of the *duende* ('a kind of undiabolic demon') that Berger found in Lorca. From Ortega y Gasset he derives the central idea of Picasso as 'a primitive man, appearing on the stage [of Europe] through the trap door [of Barcelona], a vertical invader.' Berger's Picasso is an accumulation of variously refracted historical, psychological and intuitive insights: he is made up of bits of others. He is, in the terms of Max Raphael's definition, a *caricature*: an accretion of disparate parts. It is the discordant relations and interrelations of these parts that animate Berger's Picasso. In caricature, says Raphael, 'it is the relation between . . . positive and negative elements that determine the whole – emphasizing the impossibility of there being any whole, whether a total situation, a whole man or the ensemble of their interrelations.'[8]

This insight is very close not only to Berger's method of 'constructing' Picasso but also to the conclusions he will draw from that method: the key to his positive and negative parts, his inevitable success and failure. A few lines later, Raphael observes that via the detour of caricature, great art now takes man as its subject 'not as a human being, but as a *contradictory being*, in contradiction with himself and his environment' [my emphasis][9]. In essence, this is Berger's Picasso. As mentioned earlier, Berger once commented that *Picasso* was 'written somewhat like a novel'[10] but it is a novel in which there is only this one 'contradictory being'. In place of a narrative involving several characters the 'plot' of *Picasso* involves the internal acting out of Picasso's psychological drama and the way this drama unfolds in the paintings. 'Only in fiction can we share another person's specific experiences. Outside fiction we have to generalize.' While Berger is assembling the pieces that make up Picasso, he is thought-provoking; when he tries make him move, to live, he falls back on melodrama and tautology.

The most original contribution of *Picasso*, however, lies in the precision with which 'the moment of Cubism' is located and explained. Raphael had argued that the great artistic problem handed down from the nineteenth to the twentieth century was how to combine

the dialectics of Cézanne (the relation between perceiver and perceived) and the materialism of Courbet (the physicality of things).
Berger takes up Raphael's terms and accepts his proposition but
while for Raphael 'both materialism and dialectics are completely
absent in Picasso',[11] Berger sees the Cubist paintings of 1907 to
1914 'as the only example of dialectical materialism in painting'.[12]
Raphael claims that Cubism served only to introduce a new
method of modelling and that it was only 'ostensibly' revolutionary; Berger claims that the importance of Cubism 'is almost impossible to exaggerate'. Cubism, says Berger, ushered in a
new way of seeing, it 'changed the nature of the relationships between the painted image and reality' and thus brought about 'a
revolution in the visual arts as great as that which took place in the
early Renaissance'.

One of Berger's first attempts at a project of this kind, explain-
ing the nature of 'the moment' of a particular way of painting,
deals with that period of the Renaissance with which the Cubist
revolution is most frequently compared. The questions Berger
asked in his essay 'Explanations in Purgatory' are the same as
those he will later ask of the Cubist period: 'Why were the 80 years
in Italy from about 1420 to 1500 unique in the history of European
painting? What can explain the prodigious scale and high average
quality of the art then produced. Why . . . ?' Berger's belief that the
Cubist epoch offered a 'new revolutionary truth' was similarly
longstanding, and in the late 1950s and early 1960s he was sketching out some of the ideas that would form the basis of his analysis.
The essay 'Problems of Socialist Art', as we have seen, is concerned with the 'critical question' of how to 'regard the art produced in or around Paris between about 1870 and 1920'. The essay
does not focus sharply on the Cubists – appropriately, it is im-
pressionistic – but it displays, over a slightly wider range of material, the methods and concerns of Berger's work on Cubism
itself.

We have already mentioned Berger's talent for bringing material from diverse sources into provocative proximity. Essentially,
'The Moment of Cubism' and the section on Cubism in *Picasso* are
elaborate and extended exercises in this kind of pertinent assem-
blage. His method is almost identical to the one he notices in
Marx:

Every articulation of the thought involves a connection
between opposites. Simply to call this dialectical may be to miss

the point. The words do not accumulate to confirm one another; each articulation supersedes the previous one. One might argue that this is in the nature of writing itself; in life one begins at the beginning: in literature on begins at the end. But in Marx's mode of thinking the degree to which each superseding phase of the thought modifies the orientation of the preceding phase is new, because it plays upon a new notion of discontinuity. The model is no longer an edifice constructed stone by stone or phase by phase, but a pivotal balance like that of a pair of scales or a see saw. The total of the phases no longer covers an extensive area, but instead defines a single point occupying no space at all. From paragraph to paragraph one proceeds by leaps from point to point. . . The mode of discontinuity demonstrated by Marx's thinking has now become an essential part of the modern means of communication. Discontinuity is now intrinsic to our view of reality. (*L.T.* p.85)

Berger's is a method that yields startling insights and produces breakthroughs that are denied the expert who digs a deeper trench of specialized knowledge. The danger of Berger's method is that it amasses circumstantial evidence that cannot prove, accumulates without precision, substitutes coincidences for causes and, in its eagerness to demonstrate a causal pattern, fails to distinguish between the essential and the marginal. The sheer diversity of evidence can come to suggest randomness rather than a revealed inevitability. For example, in two articles on Picasso and Velásquez by Berger published in 1961, the Cubists' concern with movement and their attempts 'to prove that space itself was a process' are linked with the advent of modern physics (especially the principles of relativity and indeterminacy) and, vaguely, with Darwin, Marx and Freud.[13]

However, in *Picasso* and in 'The Moment of Cubism', there is a perfect proportion of wood to tree. In outlining the relation between Cubism and the economic, technological, political and scientific developments of the time, Berger is not suggesting that the Cubists had necessarily even to be aware of these developments; it is enough to say that Cubism 'shared the same determinants' as these other developments. 'At the appointed time, necessities become ripe', as Kandinsky said. Berger does not want to suggest exact causality nor simple coincidence: rather, the *inevitability of coincidence*.

The extent to which this was the case in the Cubist period is powerfully confirmed by Robert Hughes. Berger, if you like, supplies the theoretical insight; Hughes reveals the way that technological and scientific breakthroughs were manifested at the level of widespread experience. In the last decade of the nineteenth century, says Hughes, the metropolis replaced the landscape as the master image of painting. The new technology of the machine age could be seen as representing 'the conquest of process':

> The machine meant the conquest of horizontal space. It also meant a sense of that space which few people had experienced before – the succession and superimposition of views, the unfolding of landscape in flickering surfaces as one was carried swiftly past it, and an exaggerated feeling of relative motion . . . due to parallax. The view from the train was not the view from the horse. It compressed more motifs into the same time. Conversely, it left less time in which to dwell on any one thing.[14]

Fast travel 'promised to telescope more experience into the conventional frame of travel' and the Eiffel Tower, built in 1889 for the Paris World Fair, was the symbol of this power of process. The most spectacular thing about the tower, however, was not seeing *it* from the ground but seeing the ground from the tower. At the time, most people, says Hughes, lived either at ground level or within 40 feet of the ground. From the tower millions of people were granted the view that had previously been available only to photographers like Nadar. They saw:

> the earth on which we live as flat, as pattern, from above. As Paris turned its once invisible roofs and now clear labyrinth of its alleys and streets towards the tourist's eye, becoming a map of itself, a new type of landscape began to seep into popular awareness. It was based on frontality and pattern, rather than on perspective recession and depth.[15]

This way of seeing was one of the pivots of human consciousness. Hughes draws up a list of earlier inventions and breakthroughs that also contributed to this sense of an accelerating rate of change; and the first artists to produce a 'convincing record' of this sense of process and transformation were, he says, the Cubists. Berger and Hughes see the moment of Cubism similarly: Berger's vision is

more diagrammatic, Hughes's less precise but vividly and auth-
entically coloured. The limitations of Berger's 'diagram' can be
seen by measuring his depiction of the Cubist moment against the
procedure for a social history of art outlined by Tim Clark in the
introductory chapter to his book, *Image of the People*. (We are
here speaking only of *Picasso*, not of 'The Moment of Cubism' in
which Berger attempts to decipher an historical moment without
relating his discoveries to a particular artist.) After listing a series
of practices to be avoided, Clark declares his own ambitions in
terms of 'a history of mediations', an attempt 'to discover what
concrete transactions are hidden behind the mechanical image of
"reflection", to know *how* "background" becomes "foreground";
instead of analogy between form and content, to discover the net-
work of real, complex relations between the two.'[16] The general
question to which this procedure tends is 'whether we can discover in the complex and specific material of a single artist's historical situation and experience the foundation of his unique subject matter and style'.[17] 'Our starting point', he goes on, 'is a certain moment of historical coalescence'. Berger's delineation of the
Cubist impulse defines such a moment, offers itself as the point
from which more detailed work can proceed.

Berger's analysis in 'The Moment of Cubism' does not simply
repeat that of *Picasso*. He once again maps out the essential coordinates but in addition places this moment in the context of the main
tradition of Western painting since the Renaissance. This tradition
is seen in terms of images which represent each of its main stages:
the art of the Renaissance is represented by a mirror; mannerism
and classicism by the theatre stage; nineteenth-century art is the
art of 'the personal account'; Cubism is the revolutionary fourth
stage which can be represented by 'the diagram'. In more detail
than in *Picasso*, Berger describes the way in which this transformation was pictorially achieved. He emphasizes that the revolution
of Cubism rested on the artists' '*intimation* of a transformed
world' [my emphasis]:

> During the first decade of this century, a transformed world
> came theoretically possible and the necessary forces of
> change could already be recognised as existing. Cubism was the
> art which reflected the possibility of this transformed world
> and the confidence it inspired. (*W.B.* p.185)

All art, Berger goes on to say, is an attempt to make unnatural the gap between the actual and the desired. 'Thus art, however free or anarchic its mode of expression, is always a plea for greater control and an example, within the artificial limits of a "medium", of the advantages of such control'. Cubism – and this is the reason Berger keeps coming back to it – is the art which most nakedly reveals this 'true' condition of art: it is the most powerful means of transformation, within a particular medium, that there has been.

Berger sees the Cubist promise as having been destroyed through the fragmenting effects of the First World War and the new kind of suffering that the war gave rise to. The limitations and typical characteristics of the de Stijl artists can be traced back to the same circumstances. In an essay entitled 'Article of Faith' Berger notes that the artists of de Stijl:

> Purified Cubism and extracted a system from it. . . But this purification took place at a time when reality was revealing itself as more tragic and far less pure than the Cubists of 1911 could ever have imagined. . . The important point is that what were still intuitively real prophecies for the Cubists became utopian dreams for the artists of de Stijl. . . De Stijl utopianism was compounded of a subjective retreat away from reality in the name of invisible universal principles. . . What is missing is an awareness of the importance of subjective experience as a historical factor. Instead, subjectivity is simultaneously indulged in and denied. The equivalent social and political mistake was to trust in economic determinism. (*A.L.* pp. 124-5)

The limitations of de Stijl, however, should not blind us to the limitations of Cubism. Although Cubism was a new and revolutionary way of seeing, it was not a complete way of seeing; there was much that could not be accomodated within its new syntax.

A few years after he wrote 'The Moment of Cubism', Berger was to draw attention to the quality of the average rather than the exceptional European oil painting. It is worth remembering that Cubism, even in the years 1907 to 1914, and even in the hands of Picasso, occasionally lacked the transforming and interrogative vigour for which Berger praises it. Peter Fuller is right when he points out that for Picasso himself there were 'areas of experience about which he felt passionately but which could never be expressed through a Cubist aesthetic'. Fuller also notes that there is

threat as well as promise in Cubist 'representations of disintegration, fragmentation, and the dissolution of the human subject,
and the physical world he inhabited'.[19] If Cubist syntax was pur-
ified into the theosophical calm of de Stijl it also, and just as easily,
merged into the maniacal restlessness of futurism and the worship
of momentum for its own sake which made it the natural servant
to, and the 'official' art of, Italian fascism. There is, as Roger
Cranshaw has noted, a naked violence in Braque's and Picasso's
Cubism. While Berger sees Cubism as embodying the powerful
optimistic energy of 'la belle epoque', Cranshaw sees Picasso's and
Braque's Cubist paintings as expressing 'the tensions and anxieties
of the "avant guerre" ':

> For a while . . . maybe from 1907, certainly from the summer of
> 1910 to the autumn of 1912, Braque and Picasso, through the
> sustained force of their violence – which was not violence at all,
> of course, but *counter-violence* – became the instruments of
> what was a very circumscribed and marginalized 'revolution',
> but one which remains the most destructive and the most
> extreme in the history of Western art.[20]

Cranshaw's tone adds to the violence he claims is already there in
Cubism but he is right in drawing attention to the impulse of self-
destruction implicit in the Cubist promise. Hence Berger's continued championship of Leger. Berger would like to create
Cubism in the image of Leger, for Leger is the most solidly optimistic, the most potentially 'durable' and least self-destructive of
Cubism's major practitioners. His is an art of solutions rather than
contradictions.

We have already mentioned that Lavin in *A Painter of our Time* is
the antithesis of Picasso. Picasso and Lavin measure each other's
success and failure. 'To be successful means being assimilated into
society, just as being a failure means being rejected.' For Berger,
the issue of success is 'an historical and not a moral one'. The experience of Picasso:

> proves that success and honour, as offered by bourgeois
> society, should no longer tempt anyone. It is no longer a
> question of refusing on principle, but of refusing for the sake of

self-preservation. The time when the bourgeoisie could offer true privileges has passed. What they offer now is not worth having. (*S.F.P.* p.206)

The issue may be historical rather than moral but it is also, for Berger, a deeply personal one. It is 1965; Berger is living in exile, poised between success and failure, between being assimilated and rejected. His verdict on Picasso serves also as a guide to his own possible future; it establishes the terms from which his ambitions can proceed and within which they can be defined and judged. Berger is explicit about his own vision of success: the example of Picasso, he says, is a failure of revolutionary nerve:

> To sustain such nerve one must be convinced that there will be another kind of success: a success which will operate in a field connecting, for the first time ever, the most complex and imaginative constructions of the human mind and the liberation of all those peoples of the world who until now have been forced to be simple, and of whom Picasso has always wished to be the representative. (*S.F.P.* p.206)

In his next book, *A Fortunate Man*, Berger's work takes an entirely new turn but his identification with the man he is writing about is even more intense than in *Picasso*.

6. A Fortunate Man

The profession's internal ideology and hierarchy attaches much higher value to highly technical performances done in exceptional cases than to in-depth work against the most widespread ills. It is as if a doctor's professional value were acknowledged by the medical profession in inverse proportion to social usefulness. . .

This contradiction between the hierarchy of professional values and the extent of social usefulness is at the root of the distortion and the unequal development of knowledge. Left to itself, any closed profession tends to give itself mandarin structures and to place its self-reproduction, the perpetuation of its privileges and power, above all other ends.

Overcoming this contradiction requires a permanent struggle not against advanced research itself, but against mandarin ideology: an ideology which claims that the holders of exceptional knowledge are responsible to their peers alone, and not to their neighbours, the people.
André Gorz

Modestly subtitled 'The Story of a Country Doctor', *A Fortunate Man* is a quiet masterpiece, a pivotal work in Berger's writing. In its combination of text and image it is also a new 'kind' of book – the only real precedent is James Agee's and Walker Evans's *Let Us Now Praise Famous Men* of 1941, a verbal and visual record of poor sharecroppers in the south of the US. Why then has *A Fortunate Man* attracted so little critical attention? Simply, I think, because it is not a work of fiction. The novel, occupying a position of extraordinary and often unwarranted prestige in our culture, is thought of as the sole location of imaginative prose. Great claims are made for formal innovation within the novel but Berger's innovativeness is of a simpler and higher order. Cultural prejudice being what it is, 'documentary' suggests a lower order of creativity than 'fiction'. Martin Amis, for example, has observed that while

Norman Mailer and Truman Capote (in *The Executioner's Song* and *In Cold Blood*) expend 'a good deal of imagination and artistry on the non-fiction form', that form necessarily 'lacks moral imagination, moral artistry. The facts cannot be arranged to give them moral point'.[1] As we shall see, the force of Berger's moral artistry makes *A Fortunate Man* a vivid refutation of Amis's thesis.

Simply on a technical level, though, *A Fortunate Man* displays all the intuitive insight, imaginative sympathy and storytelling skill of the novelist. Here is a short passage where Sassall watches a girl leave his surgery. She is depressed because her job at the laundry is intolerable; Sassall promises to do something on her behalf and then she leaves:

> Through the surgery window he saw her walking up the lane to the common, to the house in which he had delivered her sixteen years ago. After she had turned the corner, he continued to stare at the stone walls on either side of the lane. Once they were dry walls. Now their stones were cemented together. (*F.M.* p.33)

The effect of the last sentences is, as Catherine Belsey has observed, to 'call into question any generalized optimism engendered by the doctor's promise of decisive action'. Belsey goes on,

> The image of the cemented stones, naturalistically motivated but also open to metaphorical reading, suggests that stability which results from the smoothing over of differences in modern society. The reader is invited to reflect on the relationship between the fixity of this concluding *image* and the dynamic conclusion of the *story*, the doctor's alleviation of social distress in a single instance.[2]

It is easy to demonstrate that Berger has the technical skills of the novelist but it is the imaginative conception of the book as a whole that has to be considered. Berger is himself aware that his method as a writer is more subjective than is considered appropriate for a documentarist:

> What I am saying about Sassall and his patients is subject to the danger which accompanies any imaginative effort. At certain times my own subjectivity may distort. At no time can I prove

what I am saying. I can only claim that after years of observation of the subject I believe that what I am saying, despite my clumsiness, reveals a significant part of the social reality of the small area in question, and a large part of the psychological reality of Sassall's life. (*F.M.* p.110)

Psychological and social realities, documentary and imaginative intentions are dependent on each other in Berger's conception of Sassall and his relations with his patients. Sassall's position in the community is somewhere between a doctor and a priest; he is responsible for his patients' welfare rather than just their physical wellbeing; he offers guidance and advice as much as medical expertise. Above all, he offers a special kind of recognition – fraternity – to those who, through cultural deprivation, have few 'ways of recognizing themselves'. At the same time that he offers his services to the community, Sassall is aware that it is 'by virtue of the community's backwardness that he is able to practice as he does':

Their backwardness enables him to follow his cases through all their stages, grants him the power of his own hegemony, encourages him to become the 'consciousness' of the district . . . permits him to establish almost entirely on his own terms the local image of his profession. (*F.M.* p.144)

His patients' underprivilege is also the condition for what Berger sees as Sassall's almost metaphysical ambition: his 'striving towards the universal' that puts him in a 'vocational tradition' reaching back to Paracelsus and Faust. 'Driven by his need to know', Sassall is a type of the universal man whose enemy is the division of labour. Like Berger 'he is the opposite of a specialist', but the similarities between writer and doctor go beyond that. When Berger sees Sassall's life as an 'unsatisfied quest for certainty', Sassall becomes the mirrored embodiment of Berger's own working future. Sassall in his work is what Berger will become in his. More exactly, Sassall's relationship with his patients prefigures, in some ways, Berger's relationship with the peasants who are to become the subjects of *Pig Earth*. In his relationship with the foresters, Sassall seems 'like a foreigner who has become . . . the clerk of their own records.' Like Berger,

Sassall is accepted by the villagers and foresters as a man who, in the full sense of the term, lives with them. Face to face with him, whatever the circumstances, there is no need for shame or complex explanations: he will understand even when their own community as a whole will not or cannot. (*F.M.* p. 100)

A little later, Berger almost draws attention to the parallels between himself and Sassall by observing that the only other person in the area 'whose mode of thinking is comparable' with Sassall's is a writer who lives nearby. Berger explains that Sassall had not taken over the role of the parish priest, rather

He is [the villagers'] own representative ... he represents them, becomes their objective (as opposed to subjective) memory because he represents their lost possibility of understanding and relating to the outside world, and because he also represents some of what they know but cannot think. (*F.M.* p. 109)

In an interview in *Marxism Today* in 1984, Berger spoke of the effects of 'becoming' one character after another in his writing: 'storytellers lose their own identity and are open to the lives of other people.' In *A Fortunate Man* he writes of Sassall's 'imaginative "proliferation" of himself in "becoming" one patient after another'. We don't want to take this too far, to start claiming that Berger is the heart surgeon of a heartless world, but the parallels are suggestive. 'He cures others to cure himself', says Berger of Sassall. Berger writes about Sassall to write about himself.

This is not to say that Berger is writing autobiography. In many ways, as he wrestles with the problem of evaluating Sassall's work, Berger's position is the opposite of the autobiographer's: he is 'entirely at the mercy of realities [he] cannot encompass'. In place of a conclusion Berger tries to account for the impossibility of taking the measure of Sassall's endeavours. Instead of making an individual assessment of Sassall, Berger wants to see the 'historical content' of his situation, to see in Sassall's periodic bouts of depression 'what is wounding and damaging on a much larger scale'.

Berger writes best when he wants to express what he finds most difficult. His struggle to 'take the measure' of Sassall is one of his finest pieces of writing. 'I must try to be simple,' he writes:

There are such things as historical or social crises of such an order that they test all those who live through them. They are moments of truth in which, not everything, but a great deal is revealed about individuals, classes, institutions, leaders. Since the war, during the last 20 years, we have lived through a period which must be reckoned as an exact and prolonged antithesis to a moment of truth. We have exercised no choice at all.

(*F.M.* pp. 161-2)

Unaccustomed to exercizing choice, 'we find ourselves without a scale of standards for judging or accessing one another. The only standard which remains is that of personal liking – or its commercial variant, which is Personality.' And so 'we live in and accept a society which is incapable of knowing what a human life is worth'. The penultimate paragraph of the book develops this notion of momentous uncertainty:

> I do not claim to know what a human life is worth – the question cannot be answered by word but only by action, by the creation of a more just society. All that I do know is that our present society wastes and, by the slow draining process of enforced hypocrisy, empties most of the lives which it does not destroy: and that, within its own terms, a doctor who has surpassed the stage of selling cures, either directly to the patient or through the agency of a state service, is unassessable.

(*F.M.* p. 167)

What to say of these pages? Practical criticism provides a vocabulary – the rhythmic richness and weighty simplicity of the prose – but this is not enough. Nor is it enough, though it is true, to say that these pages move me. We must say why they move. They are not moving because they *appeal*, but because they offer a choice, a choice which has since been made for us. This became clear in the 1970s, particularly in the public service strikes which:

> revealed something even more distasteful about ourselves than an unwelcome confrontation with our mortality. They demonstrated something which, for the most part, we prefer to ignore – that everything has its price. Even human virtues like charity and compassion can be measured in monetary terms. The worth of unrewarded mercy, of freely given human pity, has been calculated and vested in economic functions. Caring is, after all, now a profession.[4]

Berger's difficulties in taking the measure of Sassall have since been countered with cynical ease by the logic of monetarism. Sassall, and the thousands like him for whom blood and vomit are a daily concern, are worth what they cost – and they must cost as little as possible. 'We live in and accept a society which is incapable of knowing what a human life is worth', wrote Berger. Less than 20 years later we know exactly how much the lives of miners and teachers are worth and we also know how much it is worth (in police time, redundancy payments, legal costs and hardship) to make 'them' accept 'our' assessment of their worth. A doctor is worth what he or she has to sell; those with nothing to sell are valueless. Berger's final pages move because they affirm in spite of the harsh economics that now prevail. He offers need instead of cost as guiding principal; in the face of efficient and impoverished calculus, the difficulty, the impossibility of taking the measure of Sassall become an affirmation of faith in him and in the work he does.

There is a tragic postscript to *A Fortunate Man*. *As if* overwhelmed by the shadows cast by the urgent imperatives by which he lived and worked, *as if* tormented by the uncertainties of Berger's closing pages, Sassall killed himself. Phrases of Berger's come back: 'the prolonged antithesis of a moment of truth'; 'man's worth to himself is expressed by his treatment of himself':

> A man's death makes everything certain about him. . . Death changes the facts qualitatively but not quantitively. One does not know more facts about a man because he is dead. But what one already knows hardens and becomes definite. We cannot hope for ambiguities to be clarified; we cannot hope for further change, we cannot hope for more. . . If he were dead, I would conclude this essay as death concluded his life. (*F.M.* p. 160)

In the light of Sassall's subsequent suicide, these passages become ominous. His death also explains an eerie passage in the book:

> [Sassall] is a man of extreme self-control. Nevertheless, when he was unaware of my presence, I saw him weep, walking across a field away from a house where a young patient was dying. Perhaps he was blaming himself for things done or left undone. He would transform his pain into a sense of painful

responsibility, for that is his character. (*F.M.* p.112)

When I first read this passage it struck me as odd. At the time, I assumed it to be because it is the only time in the book when we are aware of the obtrusive presence of Berger as documentarist and observer. One suddenly becomes aware, *for a moment*, of the presence of Berger and Jean Mohr, the photographer *throughout* the book. It was only when I became aware of Sassall's death that the full significance of the passage struck me. Throughout the book we are aware of the extraordinary sensitivity with which Berger responds to Sassall, with the intensity of Berger's identification with him. In this moment, however, we become aware of how much about Sassall is still unknown, of the distance between them that cannot be honestly bridged. Compare this passage with Mohr's photograph of Sassall in the door of his surgery or study – the frontispeice to the book. Sassall is framed both by the doorframe and by converging walls. We can see only a part of him and the barest fraction of the room beyond. His face is white in a beam of light. There is much that we cannot see; it is difficult to say with certainty whether he is about to step into the room and shut the door or emerge from the room and advance into the hallway. The photograph is differentiated from the passage in Berger's text by this quality of uncertainty. It is a tactful photograph; its uncertainty is the price paid for keeping its distance.

When Berger glimpses Sassall weeping, it is as though he has been looking through a private diary, as if he has glimpsed that which cannot be legitimately found out about someone else. As if, for a moment, he had profoundly invaded Sassall's privacy, so profoundly as to have glimpsed the fate of which Sassall was himself unaware.

7. *Art and Revolution*: Ernst Neizvestny

Although he has written only occasionally on sculpture, Berger puts forward his study of the Soviet sculptor Neizvestny in *Art and Revolution* as 'the best example I have achieved of what I consider to be the critical method'. Accept this claim and we can see the strengths and weaknesses of the book as representing the limitations of Berger's method. In evaluating the book we evaluate the method. As in *Picasso*, Berger begins a long way back. Russian art and its connections with the country's larger history is looked at from the time of Peter the Great to the Revolution, and from the epoch of Stalin and the purges to Neizvestny's own era of Khrushchev and the thaw. Until 1956, Berger had felt there was no option but to be pro-Soviet. In *Art and Revolution* he argues against Soviet cultural policy and endorses semi-dissident activity there. His interest in Soviet art was longstanding – but why did he choose to look at Neizvestny, a sculptor who, at the time of writing, was barely known outside the Soviet Union? To answer that we must also go back to the 1950s, to a very public quarrel.

Berger wrote on Henry Moore several times in the *New Statesman* and his dissenting voice led not only to outraged correspondence in the *Statesman* but also, on one occasion, to the British Council telephoning Moore and apologizing for Berger's review.[1] Berger made clear his reservations about Moore in a 1955 review of two new figures by the sculptor. The vision behind these works, he said, was essentially retrogressive. Of one of the carvings he wrote: 'It is a work based on an imaginative burrowing back into darkness. . . It is the very opposite of a work that aspires'. In Moore's carvings, he continued, there was no 'tension of choice': 'one accepts the shape of each invented form as one accepts that of a pebble, or as an unborn child, protected from all decision and choice, accepts the choice of its mother's womb'.[2]

In Neizvestny, Berger finds the exact antithesis of Moore. Neizvestny's maimed figures survive, in spite of their afflictions, through a pure assertion of will, 'the human power to continue'.

Neizvestny's figures fight their way into the light; they struggle to achieve the vertical.

In *Art and Revolution* itself, Berger writes that Moore's figures 'are the creatures of forces that overwhelm them'.[3] Neizvestny's figures, on the other hand, are like weightlifters, their straining assertion grows as the weight they have to defy increases. At more or less the same time that he was thinking and writing about Neizvestny, Berger wrote of Rodin's figures as 'prisoners within their own contours', of 'the terrible compression under which these figures exist'.[4] In resisting their own compression, Neizvestny's figures embody what for Berger is the essential relation of sculpture to the space that surrounds it. After a comparison of the very different kinds of spatial tension created by a tree, a crane and a bridge, Berger sees sculpture as 'totally opposed to the space that surrounds it'. Rodin's figures fail 'to create any spatial tension with their surroundings'. Neizvestny's figures fight against the space that encloses them; they resist their own confinement as if trying to break out of the materials in which they have been cast.

To praise Neizvestny's figures for resisting and to condemn Rodin's and Moore's for 'succumbing' is simply an assertion of preference. As abstractions, 'succumbing' and 'resistance' are equally meaningless; they acquire meaning and value only in relation to what is being either resisted or succumbed to. Neizvestny's sculptures give expression to his struggle against Soviet bureaucracy but, in the light of Berger's history of Soviet art, this personal struggle is the culmination *in a particular instance* of an historic one. More broadly, Neizvestny's figures have the courageous 'obstinacy of victims who resist their victimization', an ability 'to endure until they can put an end to their suffering'. Their efforts, though conceived by Neizvestny within the moulding power of Soviet history, correspond to a phase of the world struggle against imperialism. Neizvestny's sculpture is thus 'an interim monument to the endurance necessary at the beginning of this struggle'. That there are no precise connections between that struggle and Neizvestny's sculpture does not matter; the correspondence lies in the quality of effort needed to sustain that struggle – a struggle which, says Berger, is a fight 'for all human meaning'.

But Berger does not admire Neizvestny uncritically. The assertiveness that is common to much of Neizvestny's work does not encourage delicacy of observation so much as visceral surrender to its effects. However, Berger retains a delicacy and sensitivity of discrimination in the face of Neizvestny's bulking beauty; he assesses particular works according to the degree to which they fulfil their own promise. Thus the forms of *Orpheus* and *The Prophet*

> cannot contain and hold the emotions they suggest. The emotion and the meaning escape them – to importune and nag at the spectator. They are appeals rather than statements (the same is true of a great deal of modern Expressionist art) and the trouble with such appeals is that they are always addressed to an already established response. (*A.R.* p. 140)

Similarly, Berger irresistibly suggests the qualities of Neizvestny's work at its best. Sometimes his striving to capture the essential impulse of a work appears slightly ridiculous: 'the thrust and delicacy of [*Adam*] as a whole . . . suggest those sensations of density, weight, lightness, containment and flowering which are very close to the sensation of an erection'.[5] It is not a successful comparison but it *is* the product of an imaginative striving to understand the *life* of the figure. Throughout the book Berger's writing tries to make the bronze forms breathe.

Berger's prose is particularly suited to this task: in its single-mindedness of purpose it corresponds closely to Neizvestny's work. In *Art And Revolution* there is a bunched muscularity to Berger's writing; 'a clenched assertion', as one reviewer noted, 'that borders on the stammer in its fierce determination to link a given point with another'.[6]

Similarly, in one of the most perceptive essays written about Berger, David Gervais comments on the Fanon-influenced rhetoric of a passage in the book: 'The eloquence grits its teeth to contain the overwrought emotion which drives it. Hence its robot-like insistence. There is an insistence which gets in the way of our response to the thought.'[7] This insistence (or what John Spurling calls Berger's 'compulsive simplification') is one of the most striking features of Berger's style. Its essential character can be brought out most vividly by contrast. Take this passage from Linda Nochlin's discussion of realism:

> Van Eyck painting Arnolfini or Caravaggio his Magdalene, no matter how scrupulous they might have been in reproducing the testimony of visual experience, were looking through eyes, feeling and thinking with hearts and brains, and painting with

brushes, steeped in a context of belief in the reality of something other and beyond that of the mere external, tangible facts they beheld before them.[8]

Berger would say the same thing – but in the *opposite* way. His prose is constantly bracing itself for abrupt intellectual leaps. He combines emotive language and metaphor with the grammar of assertion: hence his commanding suggestiveness. This style is absolutely central to Berger's achievement. When he is looking at or reading the work of others he frequently manages to find another option, an alternative left unconsidered or hidden by the writer under consideration; his own writing, on the other hand, works by denying the reader access to an angle of insight other than his own. For exactly the reason that it sweeps objections aside so successfully, we must be suspicious of it. Spurling notes that Berger's trenchant style both grabs our attention and covers up 'abrupt surges in the argument'.[9] Gervais comments that on a first reading of *Art and Revolution* we remain passive, swept along by Berger's 'humane passion'. It is only on subsequent readings that we begin to have doubts about – for example – the ease with which Berger recruits Neizvestny under his own revolutionary banner. From here it is but a short step to what for Gervais is the crucial question to be asked of Berger's method: 'how far is Berger describing Neizvestny's imagination objectively and how far is he projecting his own imagination into it?' I spoke earlier of Berger's struggle to *become* Neizvestny's sculptures. Gervais suggests the opposite possibility: Berger's straining to make the sculptures fit his vision.

The essence of Berger's method is that it refuses the choices offered by these terms of Gervais's. How can one person describe another's imagination objectively? In an interview a few years later, Berger spoke of the critic's job as tiring because of the effort of 'projecting his imagination into the works of other people'.[10] Projecting your imagination into a work of art is not the same as imposing your prejudices on it. What is at stake is the *quality* of the imaginative projection. Criticism for Berger is the test of one imagination by another: he never 'submits' to the work of art under discussion, never surrenders to the work of art's own image of itself. Berger responds to Neizvestny as Neizvestny responded to Khrushchev, insisting, before the work of art, on discussing it as an equal. What is important for Berger is the *encounter* between artist and critic.

Such an encounter (while the artist is still alive) takes place at a specific point in the development of artist and critic. Berger was himself aware of the dangers involved in assessing Neizvestny's work at only the mid-point in the sculptor's career. Is it too soon, he asks, to try to delimit the world of Neizvestny's imagination? Nevertheless, he concludes after this moment of doubt, we can 'trace the formation of the essential Neizvestny in such a way that no future development is likely to contradict it'.

However, the main impression we get of Neizvestny's development after 1976 is of crassness. There was a hint of exactly this in some of the works discussed by Berger (when *Art And Revolution* was first published a reviewer noted that Neizvestny's sculptures were 'not impressive enough to provide a firm foundation for [Berger's] argument'[11]) but how did it come to dominate Neizvestny's work? More importantly, does Neizvestny's subsequent development invalidate Berger's main thesis and estimate of his work?

When Berger visited him in Moscow, Neizvestny worked in a cramped and dimly-lit studio. Since the famous confrontation with Khruschev, in which he told the latter, 'You may be Premier and Chairman but not here in front of my work', Neizvestny had stood in precarious relation to the Soviet authorities, tolerated but receiving few official commissions.[12] In 1969, the year in which *Art and Revolution* was published, he heard of a competition for a monument to decorate the Aswan High Dam in Egypt. Neizvestny smuggled in his entry, a design based on a lotus flower with gigantic leaves rising 270 feet into the air. He won the competition and it was a turning point in his fortunes. In the next five years he became – as he himself put it – the richest and most famous artist in the Soviet Union. This abrupt turnaround was not due *solely* to the Aswan monument; rather, the talents that the Aswan monument had abundantly displayed coincided with the needs and ambitions of the generation of technocrats and architects who came to power under Prime Minister Kosygin. There was opposition from the Academy of Art and the Artists' Union but support from powerful ministers, administrators and Party officials. Paradoxically then, Neizvestny was both working on major public commissions and being kept under close artistic and ideological scrutiny. Thus he was commissioned to decorate the new building of the Institute of Technology and Electronics in Moscow but it was not until 1974, after a two-and-a-half year battle, that he was finally given the go ahead, with only six months left to complete the project. Various other difficulties presented themselves, but with his team of collaborators Neizvestny succeeded in completing, in his own words, 'not the 900 square foot decoration that had been commissioned, but one that measured 3,000 square feet'.

Similar delays afflicted Neizvestny's bronze bust of Khruschev. Just before his death in 1971 Khrushchev had asked Neizvestny to create a monument for his grave, but it was not until three years later that the austere bronze head was finally allowed to be raised in Novodevechy cemetery. Other projects – such as the massive concrete relief designed for the new Communist Party Central Committee building in Turkmanistan – caused an outcry when they were actually completed.

Even during these years of success, then, Neizvestny felt that his ambitions were still being thwarted and that his position in the USSR was becoming increasingly untenable. In 1976, after more than 50 applications for a visa, he was allowed to emigrate to Europe. (One of the conditions of an earlier, unsuccessful application to leave was that he should denounce Berger's book; this Neizvestny refused to do.) In 1977, despite Berger's urging him to the contrary, Neizvestny moved to New York.

Since then it has emerged that all of Neizvestny's work from, he claims, the early 1960s onwards has been no more than a preparation for the project which he hopes to realize in the USA and which will represent the fullest expression of his energies and ambitions: *The Tree of Life*. Neizvestny envisages it as one of the wonders of the world, a gigantic heart rising 300 or 500 feet from the ground, a bewildering and labyrinthine monument to the diversity and history of mankind. Elevators will ferry visitors through a huge whorling spiral structure filled with 'a multitude of figures, reliefs and paintings in a variety of materials, but also with kinetic contrivances, mobiles, filmed displays, lighting effects and creative devices of all kinds'.

One thinks of Tatlin's *Monument to the Third International* – that 'unworkable, probably unbuildable metaphor of practicality'[13], as Robert Hughes called it – but Neizvestny claims that he is ready to build *his* monument; all he needs is a site and funding 'since he has long since perfected the special construction methods he intends to use'.

Since the publication of *Art and Revolution*, Neizvestny has lived under the burden of his dream; almost all his work now seems as notes towards its eventual realization. In sketchbooks, paintings and sculptures his work has been increasingly dominated by the tendencies Berger noticed in flawed works such as *Orpheus* and *The Prophet* (a reworked version of which is intended to stand at the very heart of *The Tree of Life*). Muscles bulge to no effect, robotic limbs flex mechanically. His figures of the last ten years closely resemble the superheroes of Marvel and DC comics – particularly the work of Jack Kirby in *The Fantastic Four* and *The New Gods*, John Buscema's early *Silver Surfer*, some of Jim Steranko's best work. Earlier, we compared Neizvestny's straining figures with weightlifters; his more recent figures resemble bodybuilders whose goal, as Margaret Walters astutely observes, is not action but appearance.[14] There is a static dynamism in Neizvestny's work, a kind of gluttony in the midst of power, a sense of their being (for all their power) not verbs but nouns. It is not that they are compressed by their own contours or that they fail to create a tension with their surroundings, quite the opposite: there is nothing there to resist them, they exercise a *vain* (in every sense) powerfulness against vacant opposition. The figures are still striking, but it is a result of exaggeration and not exertion.

This development in Neizvestny's work is inextricably bound up with his move to the USA:

> Neizvestny's tragedy is best understood as a Solzhenitsyn-like loss of context. In Russia he knew who he was, he knew what he was rebelling against. He was a revolutionary stretching the Soviet definition of what was acceptable as art. In New York he was just another heavy metal sculptor over-fond of crucifixions, over-reliant on dry ice effects, over-exacting on the human figure.[15]

Neizvestny's subsequent development in no way detracts from Berger's book. For Berger, the poles of Neizvestny's imagination are life and death, variously expressed in terms of endurance or surrender, advance or collapse, struggle or defeat. The essential drama of Neizvestny's figures is their struggle to triumph over the contradictions contained within them. The essence of struggle, though, is that its outcome is always uncertain – and so the essence of Neizvestny's sculpture, as seen by Berger, is that its outcome is uncertain. The dual possibilities of Neizvestny's art were already there in the sculpture *Man Restraining Himself*: 'The man is divided against himself. The division can destroy him or create him. One thigh is triumphant, the other is withered. One arm exists, the other is amputated. Such is our condition whether we recognize it or not.' The success of the sculpture depends on the uncertainty of the outcome, on the tension and balance of the oppositions being maintained: the two halves are dependent on each other. Take away the withered limbs and you are left with bravado and exhibitionism or, more generally, facile triumphalism. This has been the outcome of Neizvestny's sculptures. What was resistance in the USSR has become showy self-indulgence in the West. Uncertainty and struggle have given way to megalomaniacal certainty. As Calvino has written: 'anyone who has lived through suffering is always made of that suffering; if they try to take it away from him, he is no longer himself.'[16]

8. *G*

Berger's last two novels had been awkward failures; nothing in them could have prepared people for the masterpiece that was his next novel. As he himself said in 1972, the year of publication: 'Everything I have written has been no more than a preparation for the work of the last five years on *G*'.[1] Paying a similar tribute to the exertions involved in writing *G*, David Caute saw the athletic Mr Berger as someone who 'arriving at the stadium burdened by an abundance of talents, found himself entering simultaneously for the sprint, the mile, the shot, and the pole-vault. Performing very well at all but winning none, he finally reached a solution: *G* is the pentathlon.'[2] *G* is not only a highpoint in Berger's personal development; it is also one of the most imaginatively ambitious novels to have been published in Britain since the war.

G is born in 1888, the son of Umberto (a powerful merchant from Livorno in Italy) and his mistress Laura, an Anglo-American heiress. Umberto is already married; Laura refuses his request that she and her son come to live near him and his Italian wife. She returns to England with her child but, after becoming involved in Fabian politics, she leaves G to grow up on a farm in the country with his adult cousins Jocelyn and Beatrice. In a riding accident he knocks out his two front teeth (thus acquiring the distinctive leer that stays with him for the rest of his life) and in an obscure but frightening episode he is made to watch the apparent killing of two horses by strangers that he comes across in the middle of the night. When he is 11, in May 1898, 'the boy', as he is called, is taken to see his father in Milan and becomes caught up in the rioting and police action that preceded the establishment of parliamentary rule by Giovanni Giolitti. Three years later and back in England, 'the boy' is seduced by Beatrice. The narrative then jumps forward to September 1910, by which time the protagonist of the book is a wealthy young man who from now on, 'for the sake of convenience', is called G. He is staying in Domodossola to witness the first airborne crossing of the Alps by the Peruvian flyer, Geo

Chavez. G is vaguely connected with the flying fraternity, but while Chavez is engaged in his flight, G is preoccupied with seducing a hotel maid. From this point on, G devotes himself almost entirely to the pursuit of women. As a result of his affair with Camille Hennequin, the wife of a wealthy motor manufacturer, he is shot in the shoulder by her husband. After a brief stay in England he ends up in Trieste in 1915 on the eve of Italy's declaration of war. Trieste at that time is a hornet's nest of powerful Austrian officials, irredentists, Bosnian terrorists and spies (G himself had obtained a passport by agreeing to perform some kind of operation for the British Secret Service). He finds himself enmeshed in various political machinations which he hopes to turn to his advantage. His main concerns are seducing Marike Templemann (the wife of an Austrian banker) and Nusa, a poor Slovene working girl. In the event he seduces neither of them, deciding instead to take Nusa to a lavish ball as a calculated insult to the fiercely anti-Slovenic guests. Escaping from the uproar which he has created at the ball, he plunges into a city splitting apart with racial and political hostility. Swept along by rioters for the second time in his life, G finds himself part of a mob that is trying to burn down the offices of the Italian newspaper, *Il Piccolo*. In the ensuing confusion he is murdered on the orders of Raffaele, an Italian irredentist whose suspicions and hatred he has already aroused.

Such a summary gives little impression of the complexities of a novel whose whole conception is utterly opposed to what Lawrence Durrell called 'the sullen monorail of story and person'.[3] Like John Fowles's *The French Lieutenant's Woman*, published three years earlier, *G* is a work of conspicuous modernism, full of narrative divergences and authorial intervention. Berger is never at pains to conceal his own hand in the writing of the novel: he steps back to consider his characters, he interrupts the narrative to speak at length about his difficulties and ambitions as an author, to relate an anecdote about an incident in a Paris laundrette, to mention a letter that he has just received from a friend, or to tell of a walk through a forest. As the furious fighting in Milan is reaching its climax he breaks off abruptly:

> I cannot continue this account. . . From this point on
> everything I write will either converge upon a full stop or else
> disperse so widely that it will become incoherent. . . To stop
> here, despite all that I leave unsaid, is to admit more of the truth
> than will be possible if I bring the account to a conclusion. The

writer's desire to finish is fatal to the truth. Unity must be established in another way. (*G.* p.89)

Throughout the text quotations from others (Cézanne, Collingwood, Saint Just) and long discursive essays on disparate themes are inserted into the text without disturbing it.

Texts that stressed their own fictiveness were all the rage in the late 1960s and early 1970s, and *G* attracted a fair amount of hostility for its excessive trendiness in this respect. For Graham Lord in the *Sunday Express, G* was a 'trendy mockery of a novel'; Auberon Waugh in the *Spectator* devoted a page and a half to considering the 'Critical Questions of the Utmost Importance' raised by Berger's 'imbecilic' book.[4] Even David Caute, in a long, sensitive review on the front page of the *Times Literary Supplement*, complained of Berger 'employing and rather overtaxing many of the devices used in recent years by Sarraute, Sollers, Butor and the other novelists who have said farewell to naturalistic certainty and divinely certified mimesis.'[5]

Hence, he concludes, 'one comes away from *G* as from many modern paintings: provoked and stimulated, yet baffled and vaguely resentful'. In *The Situation of the Novel*, Bernard Bergonzi quotes Caute's conclusion as confirmation of his own assessment: 'vivid in its local detail but self-indulgent and indefensibly baffling in its total effect'.[6]

Nothing dates more quickly than the frantically up-to-date but today's readers are unlikely to be either troubled or bored by what Caute called devices (suggesting gimmicky interventions or superfluous additions to the text) but which are better seen as an integral part of the whole conception of the work. Besides, all of Berger's artistic ambition and integrity mitigate against pointless ingenuity and gratuitous experimentation. Caute's invocation of Sarraute *et al* is, nevertheless, illuminating. W.H. Auden writes somewhere of how, after reading E.M. Forster's chapter on Gide's *Counterfeiters* in *Aspects of the Novel*, he was desperately excited at the prospect of reading the novel. *Counterfeiters* itself proved to be a great disappointment and I suspect that Auden's encounter with Gide is true of many readers of a later generation who are attracted to the *nouveau roman*: excitement rapidly evaporating into a steam of tedium.

Writing of the pioneering work of Picasso, Braque, Gris and so on in his essay 'Problems of Socialist Art', Berger commented that 'their studios were somewhat like laboratories, from which the traffic of life was excluded. Their attitude of mind was a little like that of pure mathematicians.'' The early Cubists forged a new language but, Berger goes on: 'This new language could only become vital when applied to themes and conclusions drawn from deep human experience rather than purely theoretical analysis'.[8] The Zadkine monument in Rotterdam is such a vital work of art; its relation to Cubism is the same as *G*'s relation to the more mathematical experiments of the *nouveau roman*. Berger's primary concern is not an assault on the realist text: it is in telling a story in a new way – in such a way that the conception of what constitutes a narrative or story is changed.

In the 1950s, Berger's political campaign for realism against abstract expressionism was partly determined by the absence of a Marxist modernism in this country. The conspicuous modernism of *G* is less an abandonent of realist principles than an attempt to achieve a Marxist modernism that represents both a higher stage in the evolution of broadly-defined realism and a formal resolution of the problem of commitment. The distinction between realism and other modes of expression, writes Berger in *Art and Revolution*,

> can only be made in a given historical context by reckoning the possible complexity of any imaginable totality at that moment. Realism is not a fixed measure but a variable and comparative achievement. . . The most complex totality which man could once imagine was God. Realism is the attempt to grasp that totality in terms of man: man with his 'stolen essence' – as Feuerbach defined God – restored to him. (*A.R.* p.52)

G then is anti-naturalist not in the interests of a displacement of 'reality' but in the interests of a more exact rendering of that reality. Here the reference to the Cubists becomes extremely important. A brief reminder of Berger's analysis of the Cubist method will be useful: with its stress on interconnection, he noted, Cubism combined a multiplicity of viewpoints 'to arrive at a far more complex image of reality'. Cubist art was concerned with process rather than state, with interaction between objects rather than with objects as entities in themselves. Forms were dislocated to show moments of change and the spectator, rather than passively receiving the ordering of reality through perspective, had actively to construct it from the complexity of these forms. In short, the essential aspect of Cubism 'is to deny a single definition of reality and replace it with a multiple interpretation'.[9]

Now *G* is not a programmatic 'Cubist novel' – but it is worth remembering that *G*'s adult life coincides almost exactly with the pioneering years of Cubism and that it is easy to find literary equivalents for most of the effects described above. Conventional narrative is the equivalent of classical perspective, dislocation of narrative corresponds to dislocation of pictorial form; for 'objects' we can read story or characters. At times there is a strikingly close parallel between the verbal effects of Berger and the visual effects of Braque and Picasso:

> Whom were we walking?
> I was a knee which wanted the thigh on the other leg.
> The sounds of my most tender words were in your arse.
> Your heels were my thumbs.
> My buttocks were your palms.
> I was hiding in one corner of your mouth. You looked for me there with your tongue. There was nothing to be found.
> With your throat swollen, my feet in the pit of my stomach, your legs hollow, my head tugging at your body, I was your penis. (*G*. p.228)

> It was as if his mind had been turned into a hall of mirrors in which, although all the reflections moved together, each represented something different. (*G*. p.332)

The effortless transition from first to third person narrative achieves the same sense of dislocated harmony that we find in Cubism. There is even, in the way that direct speech, never indicated by inverted commas, merges into narrative (to the extent that it is sometimes difficult to tell who is speaking), an equivalent of the way that objects merge into and become indistinguishable from the painted surface of the picture. In its freeze-frame intensity *G*'s short epigrammatic sections achieve the same 'mixing of the successive and the simultaneous' of Cubism.[10]

Cubism was not simply a formal innovation; it was the quintessentially modern way of seeing: the most appropriate vehicle for modern experience. An essential aspect of the Cubist moment was summed up by A.N. Whitehead:

> The misconception which has haunted philosophic literature throughout the centuries is the notion of independent existence. There is no such mode of existence. Every entity is

only to be understood in terms of the way in which it is interwoven with the rest of the universe.[11]

'Never again', writes Berger, 'will a single story be told as though it were the only one'. Every story, in other words, can be understood in terms of the way in which it is interwoven with history. The story of G cannot be understood simply through its unfolding in time. It must be seen *across* time in its inextricable relationship with simultaneous events. The solitary unity of linear narrative is inadequate. 'Unity must be established in another way.' Berger commented on exactly this in his essay 'The Changing View of Man in the Portrait':

> We hear a lot about the crisis of the modern novel. What this involves, fundamentally, is a change in the mode of narration. It is scarcely any longer possible to tell a straight story sequentially unfolding in time. And this is because we are too aware of what is continually traversing the story-line laterally. That is to say, instead of being aware of a point as an infinitely small part of a straight line, we are aware of it as an infinitely small part of an infinite number of lines, as the centre of a star of lines. Such awareness is the result of our constantly having to take into account the simultaneity and extension of events and possibilities.
>
> There are many reasons why this should be so; the range of modern means of communication; the scale of modern power; the degree of personal political responsibility that must be accepted for events all over the world, the fact that the world has become indivisible; the unevenness of economic development within that world; the scale of the exploitation. All these play a part. Prophecy now involves a geographical rather than historical projection; it is space, not time, that hides consequences from us. To prophesy today it is only necessary to know men as they are throughout the whole world in all their inequality. Any contemporary narrative which ignores the urgency of this dimension is incomplete and acquires the over-simplified character of a fable. (*L.T.* p.40)

Traditionally, the novel is concerned with personal relationships and personal morality. The historical novel, however, seeks to show the interrelations of these individuals with history and one critic, Shirley Toulson, sees Berger as continuing the work of the great historical novels of the nineteenth century: 'In this chronicle, Berger has set himself the vast task that Tolstoy undertook: that of depicting how each one of us is history in that we are both monumentally shaped by events and, in small measure, by the mere act of inhabiting our skins, influence their course.'[13]

The invocation of Tolstoy's name does not get us very far; Berger's similarities with the Russian master are more likely to confuse than illuminate. In the same way that *The French Lieutenant's Woman* is the novel that John Fowles's Victorian predecessors could not write, Berger in *G* is undertaking something that Tolstoy could *not* have written. As Robbe-Grillet asked in *Notes Towards a New Novel* (1963): 'Why bother to write in a form whose great masters cannot be surpassed?' Like Fowles, Berger is writing an entirely new kind of historical novel; his endeavours owe more to Marx than to Tolstoy. It is to Marx that the book owes its special kind of unity, a unity which 'plays upon a new notion of discontinuity' and which has 'become an essential part of the modern means of communication'. In a key passage of the novel, Berger explains his method in detail:

> Some say of my writing that it is too overburdened with metaphor and simile: that nothing is ever what it is but is always like something else. This is true, but why is it so? Whatever I perceive or imagine amazes me by its particularity. The qualities it has in common with other things – leaves, a trunk, branches, if it is a tree: limbs, eyes, hair, if it is a person – appear to me to be superficial. I am deeply struck by the uniqueness of each event. From this arises my difficulty as a writer – perhaps the magnificent impossibility of my being a writer. How am I to convey such uniqueness? . . . I have little sense of unfolding time. The relations which I perceive between things – and these often include causal and historical relations – tend to form in my mind a complex synchronic pattern. I see fields where others see chapters. And so I am forced to use another method to try to place and define events. A method which searches for co-ordinates extensively in space, rather than consequentially in time. I write in the spirit of a geometrician. One of the ways in which I establish co-ordinates extensively is by likening aspect with aspect, by way of metaphor. I do not wish to become a prisoner of the nominal, believing that things are what I name them. (*G* p. 152)

Caute takes Berger's limited 'sense of unfolding time' as a partial explanation of what he feels is the lack of a 'certain dramatic urgency' in Berger's novels. This may be true of *The Foot of Clive* or *Corker's Freedom* but it is not true of *G* where the lack of narrative 'rush' creates a great gain in dramatic intensity. The lack of, or rather, Berger's inability to sustain, patiently unfolding naturalistic scenes means that all attention is concentrated into short 'stanzas' of prose isolated from each other by wide spaces on the page. This combines with a predilection for didactic and epigrammatic assertion to enable Berger to move effortlessly between two apparently distinct discursive levels: essay and fiction. Digression and speculation can be inserted into the text without interrupting or disturbing it.

These comments were suggested by Fredric Jameson's discussion of Proust in *Marxism and Form*. His conclusion can be accurately applied to Berger: 'the result of this rather static organization, initially determined by a storytelling *deficiency* in imagination, is a more complex rendering of the passage of time than had hitherto been possible in conventional linear narration.'[13]

The arrangement of the 'stanzas' of *G* bears a formal resemblance to Walter Benjamin's 'Theses on the Philosophy of History'. In fact the resemblance is more than formal; Benjamin's suggestive theses are close to the theoretical driving force behind Berger's fictional method.[14]

Quoting from Collingwood, Berger notes that 'all history is contemporary history', that past events should 'vibrate in the historian's mind'. Likewise, G himself finds 'it impossible to separate one memory from another . . . the effect was the opposite of what memory usually does'. G is 'oppressed by the abundance of his memories'; he feels 'condemned to live even the present in the past tense'. G's sense of biographical simultaneity is the fictional embodiment of Berger's own lack of a sense of 'unfolding time', his sense of the contemporaneity of history. The similarity to some of Benjamin's 'Theses' is striking. Benjamin:

> 'To articulate the past historically does not mean to recognize it "the way it really was" (Ranke). It means to seize hold of a memory as it flashes up at a moment of danger. Historical materialism wishes to retain that image of the past which unexpectedly appears to man singled out by history at a moment of danger.'[15]

The awareness that they are about to make the continuum of history explode is characteristic of the revolutionary classes at the moment of their action. . .[16]

Berger:

At the barricades the pain is over. The transformation is complete. It is completed by a shout from the rooftops that the soldiers are advancing. Suddenly there is nothing to regret. The barricades are between their defenders and the violence done to them throughout their lives. There is nothing to regret because it is the quintessence of their past which is now advancing against them. On their side of the barricades it is already the future.

Every ruling minority needs to numb and, if possible, to kill the time sense of those whom it exploits by proposing a continuous present. This is the authoritarian secret of all methods of imprisonment. The barricades break that present. (G p.84)

The quote from G is not, of course, the only point where Berger's novel is indebted to Benjamin; it is cited because it offers precise echoes of Benjamin's phrasing. Benjamin's method is the most lyrical and extreme example of the unity in discontinuity, the leaping from point to point and paragraph to paragraph that Berger noted in Marx. G represents the complete utilization in fictional form of that dialectical method. It is not an historical novel in the Tolstoyan sense, but a novel which seeks to liberate fiction from its hostility to the claims of theory by combining them in a new imaginative totality.

One other aspect of the structuring and conception of G must be briefly noted: the influence of film and writing for film. Many of the effects in G are strikingly cinematic:

TWO MEN.
Descending to the house at dusk through the wood above the beech trees. An Autumn evening. Puddles. A red sky. Smoke rising straight from the chimneys. The wooden noise of a pigeon flying from one copse to another. Cold rising from the ground: now at waist level. (G pp.55-6)

More specifically, the unique structuring and scenic arrangement of *G* owes something to Godard. Consider Susan Sontag on Godard:

> Instead of narration unified by the coherence of events (a 'plot'), the narrative of Godard's films is regularly broken or segmented by the incoherence of events and by abrupt shifts in tone and level of discourse. Events appear to the spectator partly as converging toward a story, partly as a succession of independent tableaux.[17]

The *tone* of a Godard film is very different to Berger's novel but the mode of imagination is strikingly similar. Another passage from Sontag is even more pertinent in the light of Berger's own comments on his method (his attempts to establish a unity that is not based on the idea of an 'end') and in the light of the abrupt death of G at the end of the novel: 'The horizon is the straight bottom edge of a curtain arbitrarily and suddenly lowered upon a performance'. Sontag:

> Each film remains a fragment in the sense that its possibilities of elaboration can never be used up. For, granted the acceptability, even desirability, of the method of juxtaposition ('I prefer simply putting things side by side') . . . there can indeed be no internally necessary end to a Godard film. . . Every film must either seem broken off abruptly or else ended arbitrarily – often by the violent death of one or more of the main characters.[18]

What of G? We know his history but almost nothing about him. There is probably no novel of comparable length in which the principal protagonist speaks so few lines (what few lines there are amount to little more than blank expressions of politeness). He is felt as a powerful physical presence but communicates nothing about himself. When he meets Donato and Raffaele towards the end of the novel they speak of his sharing their dream. 'You are wrong', replies G, 'I am not a dreamer.'[19] When Weymann asks him what he does G replies: 'I travel'. 'The answer was neither superficial nor evasive. The constant stranger must continually travel'.[20] When Hennequin shoots him, G is as indifferent to the prospect of his own death as he had been to Chavez's. He uses his wealth but seems indifferent to it. He becomes embroiled in political events but never attempts to fathom their significance. He is radically immune to all morality: 'To morality there are no mysteries. That is why there are no moral facts, only moral judgements. Moral judgements require continuity and predictability. A new, profoundly surprising fact cannot be accomodated by morality.' (G p.222)

Since he grows up without father or mother, G's impersonality is built into his biography.[21] His early life is dominated by two women (named after the heroines of Petrarch and Dante: Laura and Beatrice); he then falls in love with a governess, and is later seduced by Beatrice. In all his adult life, his sole motivation seems to be sexual: 'His desire, his only aim was to be alone with a woman. No more than that.' The principal impression of his sexual adventures is of icily determined purpose. None of the women he sleeps with find out who he is – except, possibly, Marika: 'Who are you really?' she asks him. 'You are not who you say you are. . . Who are you really?' G replies: 'Don Juan.'[22] It is an important moment in the book.

The germ of the idea that was to become G grew out of Picasso when Berger was drawn to think of Picasso as a type of Don Juan in relation to art. While he was working on the novel, he referred to it as a book about Don Juan in 1900 ('I do not know whether it will be eventually categorized as an essay, a novel, a treatise, or the description of a dream').[23] 'G' stands for Giovanni (the names Don Juan and Don Giovanni are interchangeable) and a more specific point of reference for the novel is Mozart's opera; not so much in terms of the similarities of plot (a duel, jealous rivals, the inviting of a peasant girl, Zerlina, to the opera) as in Kierkegaard's response to the opera and the character of Don Juan. It is Kierkegaard's essay 'The Immediate Stages of the Erotic' in Either/Or Volume 1 that provides the key to our understanding of G.

For Kierkegaard, Don Giovanni is Mozart's supreme achievement, the greatest of all operas. Mozart's hero is the perfect embodiment of the type of Don Juan who, says Kierkegaard, 'constantly hovers between being the idea, that is to say, energy, life – and being the individual'.[24] It is in 'this generality, in this floating between being an individual and being a force of nature' that the essence of Don Juan is to be found. He is 'an individual who is constantly being formed, but who is never finished' and in his unending quest he resembles another great archetype: Faust. His sexual quest is an absolute one; he desires absolutely: 'His love is not psychical but sensual, and sensual love, according to his conception, is not faithful, but absolutely faithless; he loves not one but all, that is to say, he seduces all. He exists only in the moment.'[25]

Everything for Don Juan 'is a matter of the moment only. To see her and to love her, that was one and the same'. He is a 'sensual genius and the object of his desire is 'the sensual, the sensual alone'.

The similarities between Kierkegaard's conception of Don Juan and Berger's own hero are striking, particularly their 'floating' between being idea and individual, their experience of desire as an almost existential absorption in the present.

John Fowles has commented that in *The French Lieutenant's Woman* he tried 'to show an existential awareness before it was chronologically possible.'[26] The existential principles at work in *G* are more clearly defined. In an interview, Berger once said that *G* was 'about the nature of freedom'; more precisely it is concerned with the possibility of sexual freedom: 'That is the only poem to be written about sex – here, here, here – now'.[27] At this point we need to distinguish between a Casanova and a Don Juan.

A Casanova is debauched, a sexual glutton whose goal is satiety; he is a cunning seducer, insatiable because he seeks pleasure after pleasure. Don Juan's desire is absolute; this is why, as Kierkegaard noted, he is insatiable. Casanova takes his pleasure from others; Don Juan seems to *offer* something. *G*, Berger seems to be saying, offers the women he seduces the *possibility* of revelation, of liberation – though this freedom may be illusory and temporary. Expanding on his conception of *G* as a type of Don Juan, Berger once described him as 'a man who fucks to destroy society in his own mind. . . He only occurs at certain historical moments, at other historical moments that same man could be a revolutionary.'[28]

G's actions then are indistinguishable from the philanderer but his determination to pursue his own ends in the face of social convention is disruptive, subversive; his consciousness is revolutionary. At another time his initial could have stood for Garibaldi (as *G* was actually nicknamed when at school; and perhaps the flyer, Geo Chavez, represents another of the possibilities latent in *G*'s character). As it is, there is no political outlet for *G*'s revolutionary consciousness. In his fate we glimpse the conflagration that is soon to swamp Europe. Like the revolutionary promise of Cubism, the subversive potential of *G* is overwhelmed by the clash of Imperial powers.

The historical moment of the Don Juan, as conceived by Berger, comes when a society is stagnant, where every channel for change is blocked. Only, as Berger himself has commented, where women are the undisputed property of men – where men act and women appear – is he a subversive force. He cannot flourish where women are themselves struggling for emancipation since his promise is, ultimately, an intense expression of patriarchal power. In other words, he is dependant on the social organization of gender which his mere presence seems to threaten; he depends on women's powerlessness, on their not recognizing him as a representative of the power he cannot but exploit. And at this point, especially from a 1980s vantage point, the distinction between a Don Juan and a Casanova collapses.

Despite the hostility of many of the reviewers, in November 1972, *G* won the Booker Prize for fiction (followed by the *Guardian* Fiction Prize and the James Tait Black Memorial Prize). In those days the Booker Prize money was £5,000 and at the award dinner Berger announced that half the money would be used to research his next book – a study of migrant labour – and the other half would be donated to the Black Panthers. The following is an edited extract from his speech:

> Since you have awarded me this prize, you may like to know, briefly, what it means to me.
>
> The competitiveness of prizes I find distasteful. And in the case of this prize, the publication of the short list, the deliberately publicised suspense, the speculation of the writers concerned as though they were horses, the whole emphasis on winners and losers is false and out of place in the context of literature.
>
> Nevertheless prizes act as a stimulus – not to writers themselves but to publishers, readers and booksellers. And so the basic cultural value of a prize depends upon what it is a stimulus to. To the conformity of the market and the consensus of average opinion; or to imaginative independence on the part of both reader and writer. If a prize only stimulates conformity, it merely underwrites success as it is conventionally understood. It constitutes no more than another chapter in a success story. If it stimulates imaginative independence, it encourages the will to seek alternatives. Or, to put it very simply, it encourages people to question. Yet one does not have to be a

novelist seeking very subtle connections to trace the five thousand pounds of this prize back to the economic activities from which they came. Booker McConnell have had extensive trading interests in the Caribbean for over 130 years. The modern poverty of the Caribbean is the direct result of this and similar exploitation. One of the consequences of this Caribbean poverty is that hundreds of thousands of West Indians have been forced to come to Britain as migrant workers. Thus my book about migrant workers would be financed from the profits made directly out of them or their relatives and ancestors.

More than that, however, is involved. The industrial revolution, and the inventions and culture which accompanied it and which created modern Europe, was initially financed by profits from the slave trade. And the fundamental nature of the relationship between Europe and the rest of the world, between black and white, has not changed. In *G* the statue of the four chained Moors is the most important single image of the book. This is why I have to turn this prize against itself. And I propose to do so by sharing it in a particular way. The half I give away, will change the half I keep.

First let me make the logic of my position really clear. It is not a question of guilt or bad conscience. It certainly is not a question of philanthropy. It is not even, first and foremost, a question of politics. It is a question of my continuing development as a writer: the issue is between me and the culture which has formed me.

Before the slave trade began, before the European de-humanized himself, before he clenched himself on his own violence there must have been a moment when black and white approached each other with the amazement of potential equals. The moment passed. And henceforth the world was divided between potential slaves and potential slavemasters. And the European carried this mentality back into his own society. It became part of his way of seeing everything.

The novelist is concerned with the interaction between individual and historical destiny. The historical destiny of our time is becoming clear. The oppressed are breaking through the wall of silence which was built into their minds by their oppressors. And in their struggle against exploitation and neo-colonialism – but only through and by virtue of this common struggle – it is possible for the descendants of the slave and the slavemaster to approach each other again with the amazed hope of potential equals.

This is why I intend to share the prize with those West Indians in and from the Caribbean who are fighting to put an end to their exploitation. The London-based Black Panther movement has arisen out of the bones of what Bookers and other companies have created in the Caribbean; I want to share this prize with the Black Panther movement because they resist both as black people and workers the further exploitation of the oppressed. And because, through their Black People's Information Centre, they have links with the struggle in Guyana, the seat of Booker McConnell's wealth, in Trinidad and throughout the Caribbean: the struggle whose aim is to expropriate all such enterprises.

You know as well as I do that the amount of money involved – as soon as one stops thinking of it as a literary prize – is extremely small. I badly need more money for my project about the migrant workers of Europe. The Black Panther movement badly needs money for their newspaper and for their other activities. But the sharing of the prize signifies that our aims are the same. And by that recognition a great deal is clarified. And in the end – as well as in the beginning – clarity is more important than money.'

At the time, the controversy over the prize money embittered and blinded critics to the worth of the novel. Now, with the passage of time, we can take a more balanced account of Berger's achievement and see G as the modernist masterpiece that it is.

9. *Ways of Seeing*

1972 was also the year in which *Ways of Seeing* first appeared. It began as a series of four inexpensive television programmes conceived as a riposte to Kenneth Clark's massively ornate and extremely expensive *Civilization*. 'Eleven countries and 117 locations visited; works in 118 museums and 18 libraries shown', boasted the press release for *Civilization*. Where Clark the connoisseur observed the triumphal progress of great art through the centuries, Berger the materialist aimed to shatter Clark's authority by demonstrating some of the illusions on which the authority of art was based in the second half of the twentieth century.

The central concern of the project – the series of programmes and the book based on the series – was to consider the effects that mass reproduction had had on art, to develop the themes, as Berger indicates, of Walter Benjamin's essay, 'The Work of Art in the Age of Mechanical Reproduction'. Benjamin had claimed that the 'aura' of the work of art – a product of its unique existence in a single place – had been destroyed by the advent of mechanical reproduction which made possible the detachment of the work of art from its place in ritual and tradition. Berger was not the first to expand on Benjamin's prophetic insights. In *Voices of Silence*, first published in English in 1954, André Malraux had advanced the idea that the abundance of reproduced images constituted a constantly circulating museum-without-walls, a *musée imaginaire*, that was available to everyone at the cost of the loss of the original context of the work of art. A more immediate precedent for Berger was Edgar Wind's 'The Mechanization of Art', the 1960 Reith lecture that looked at the ways in which mass reproduction changed both the world and – since the fact of reproducibility was now stamped on artists' minds – the nature of art itself.[1]

More generally, *Ways of Seeing* was a response to what Harold Rosenberg termed 'the reign of the art market', the calculation of aesthetic value in terms of its cash equivalent. This was a comparatively new situation. Even in 1950, it would not have been possible to predict the stranglehold that the market would come to exert over modern art from the 1960s onwards, when dealers and auction houses began aggressively to create a booming art market. Increasing interest in art investment and rising prices worked together to produce a self-generating inflationary spiral. The function of the work of art by the 1970s was 'simply to sit on the wall and get more expensive'.[2] The colossal endowments of institutions like the Getty Museum have meant that paintings are now, in the 1980s, more valuable than ever, so that the function of paintings has changed since the 1970s; now many of the world's masterpieces do not hang on walls and get more valuable, they lie in bank vaults and perform the same task in safer obscurity.

The series *Ways of Seeing* was first broadcast in the Spring of 1972 on BBC2 late in the evening. The audience was small but since the 'switch-off rate' was extraordinarily low (i.e. once people began watching they continued till the end), the makers of the series were able to persuade the BBC to broadcast it again at prime time. The influence of the series and the book that Berger wrote after this hesitant start was enormous. Throughout the 1970s it was the key text in art colleges in Britain and in the USA; for many students and teachers alike it represented a turning point in their thinking about art. It opened up for general attention areas of cultural study that are now commonplace – decoding advertisements, for example – but which in 1972 were either virtually unknown or existed only in embryonic stage within the academy. (Many of the ideas of the series had already appeared in articles and essays by Berger: it is the transition to television and best-selling paperback that is important.)* Taken together as Peter Fuller has said, the series and the book have had 'a greater influence than any other art critical project of the last decade', and probably, I would add, of the post-war period.[3]

If the book does not now occupy quite the canonical place that it once did that is partly due to the immensity of its influence. In the first place, there is a virtually automatic reaction against a book that achieves immediate notoriety. *Ways of Seeing* is often remembered with Marshall McLuhan's *The Medium is the Massage* as a book central to its time but marginal to our own. Such an impression is suggested by the overall design of the book with its

---

* See 'The Historical Function of the Museum', 'The Changing View of Man in the Portrait', 'Art and Property Now', 'Nude in a Fur Coat' and, most vitally, 'Past Seen from a Possible Future'.

photographic essays and the use throughout of bold caption type.

Secondly, although no single book has the suggestive range of *Ways of Seeing*, its individual parts have been improved upon by its direct and indirect successors. 'Our principal aim has been to start off a process of questioning' writes Berger; the book offers no more than 'a project for study' that should 'be continued by the reader'. It is the fate of all good teachers to be outdone by their pupils; *Ways of Seeing* has been improved on, but this is an indication of the way in which it fulfilled its own ambitions.

A central weakness of the book is its lack of precision, detail and academic thoroughness. These inadequacies have to be noticed and improved upon but the fact that *Ways of Seeing* largely supplied the vocabulary for these criticisms to be made and that its purpose was primarily polemical, is even more important – as is the fact that it is not Berger's work alone. Since 1972, most people's contact has been with the book rather than the series and so the tendency to identify *Ways of Seeing* solely with Berger has steadily increased. Berger himself has always emphasized that this was a collaborative venture and has repeatedly drawn attention to the essential contribution of the producer /director, Mike Dibb. Dibb is one of the most remarkable and original film makers working in television and *Ways of Seeing* is, above all, superb television. Even now, 15 years later, the programmes are startling; the only things to have dated are Berger's haircut and shirt (this was 1972 when everyone looked like a first-division footballer).

Dibb (or more accurately the *Ways of Seeing* team) has a masterly control of visual argument. More than that, argument is turned into compelling narrative. Ideas are enacted rather than simply explained. Sound and vision tug at each other, coaxing extra significances and nuances out of one another. You watch in a state of perpetual expectation which is simply another phrase for active absorption – following clues instead of being led by the nose. The book can give little sense of the visual richness of the programmes. The relation of book to series is, to exaggerate slightly, that of a prose translation of a poem to the original. In another sense though, as John Walker has noted, the different versions of *Ways of Seeing* illustrate Berger's central thesis, that, in an age of mass reproduction, the same material makes itself available in diverse forms.[4]

The extent to which Berger's commentary in the programmes differs from the text of the book is surprising. Programme One begins abruptly with a pre-credit sequence that symbolically establishes the series' iconoclastic designs: Berger walks up to Botticelli's *Venus and Mars*. It is framed, the original we assume. He cuts out Venus's head, turning it into a head-and-shoulders portrait of a young woman. The camera focuses on this image before following it, with rapid editing, through the process of mass reproduction until hundreds of identical postcards of the image begin to pour from the presses. The argument of this first programme is substantially the same as in the first part of the book but much of it unfolds visually rather than verbally. If Berger's commentary is didactic and polemical, the camerawork and editing are deft and suggestive. The images on the screen contain the argument, they do not decorate it: a film unfolds in time in a way that a painting does not, says Berger, and the camera stares steadily at Breughel's *Procession to Calvary*. The canvas is teaming with life and movement but at this distance, on the TV screen, we cannot decipher it satisfactorily. As we become impatient with peering into this too-distant canvas Berger's commentary resumes: 'You have been waiting impatiently for the camera to move in and examine details. . .' The camera moves in, turning the Breughel into filmic narrative, turning parts into whole. Details from Caravaggio's *Last Supper* are singled out, first with background music from an Italian opera giving the painting melodramatic urgency; then with a religious chorale which gives the painting the hushed intensity of religious awe.

Goya's *The Third of May* appears on screen. Arguing that images now have only diminished authority over their meaning, Berger asks us to imagine that we have been watching another channel and that we see the Goya after turning over. On screen are girls dancing to a pop song – cut back to the Goya. Then we go from Goya to 'another channel' and see a black guerilla fighter being executed. Then we switch channels, back to the Goya whose meaning has been shifted back and forth by the power of these juxtapositions. (Godard has also attempted a startling experiment with this painting in his recent film, *Passion*: the painting is 'modelled' by actors and the camera moves around them until it shares the viewpoint of those about to be executed, staring down the barrels of the loaded rifles.) These examples are fairly schematic, the point is that the programmes are made up of dozens of visual felicities that work effortlessly and powerfully on the viewer.

The seductive first programme ends with a comment from Berger that serves as an answer in anticipation of subsequent criticism. Remember, he says, that 'I am controlling and using for my own purposes the means of reproduction needed for these programmes. I hope you will consider what I arrange – *but be sceptical of it*'.

Of course this is a rhetorical ploy – be sceptical so that you may be more thoroughly convinced – but perhaps the book of *Ways of Seeing* suffers from having to state firmly what the programmes could suggest. This important difference between series and book can be seen easily in the way that they introduce their respective arguments. On screen, Berger announces quite simply that in the age of technical reproduction we see the paintings of the past differently, 'and if we understand why this is so we shall understand something about ourselves'. The book begins with the more epic pronouncement that: 'Seeing comes before words. The child looks and recognizes before it can speak'. This has all the resonance of the genuinely empty claim. Compare it with Raymond Williams's earlier but similarly epigrammatic suggestion that 'we learn to see a thing by learning to describe it.'[5] Epigrams have an automatic authority as condensed truths but that authority can be tested by expanding them, by writing them out in longhand, as it were.

Significantly, Berger's claim rests epigraphically on its own as an unconnected claim which, fortunately, has little bearing on what follows. Williams, on the other hand, continues: 'this is the normal process of perception, which can only be seen as complete when we have intercepted the incoming sensory information either by a known configuration or rule, or by some new configuration which we can try to learn as a new rule'. In saying that we see by learning to describe, Williams relates 'seeing to communication in a fundamental way' and suggests the 'social construction of reality', as it came to be known. Berger's claim ignores the fact that while we might open our eyes and *see* before we can speak, we cannot *recognize* without a socially acquired grammar of visual perception. As he had himself hinted in *Picasso*, 'the eye can only develop as fast as one's understanding of the objects seen.'[6]

The opening assertion is not the only place in the book where Berger is guilty of distorting simplification: his claim that 'reproduction makes the meaning of a work of art ambiguous', for example, carries with it the suggestion that *before* mass reproduction a painting's meaning was unambiguous and unique. Was a work of art really as solid and unshakeable in its meaning as this suggests? Did heated debate over the meaning of works of art not exist well before the invention of the camera? The way that technical experimentation by artists combined with the sociopolitical phenomenon of Renaissance Humanism and led gradually to the development of scientific perspective is glossed over in these terms:

> The convention of perspective, which is unique to European art and which was first established in the early Renaissance, centres everything on the eye of the beholder. It is like a beam from a lighthouse – only instead of light travelling outwards, appearances travel in. The conventions called those appearances *reality*. Perspective makes the single eye the centre of the visible world. Everything converges on to the eye as to the vanishing point of infinity. The visible world is arranged for the spectator as the universe was once thought to be arranged for God. (*W.S.* p. 16)

Berger then goes on to claim that with the invention of the camera everything changed, an assertion which overstates the importance of technological change *in isolation from* the social base of that change. Elsewhere, he substitutes a cryptic conspiracy of the ruling class ('fear of the present leads to mystification of the past') for the more complex workings of cultural hegemony.

To have addressed each of these questions adequately, particularly the problem of the development of perspective, would have required the longest-running 'arts' programme ever made. However, the problem that remains is one of tone. In each of these instances we know what Berger *means* and the initial reaction of the reader is likely to be one of startled admiration. Our subsequent doubts are the price Berger must pay for the extra polemical clout his colourful metaphors and unqualified assertions give to the text.

Peter Fuller's *Seeing Berger: A Revaluation* is the most accessible and widely available critique of *Ways of Seeing*, and in considering the central theses of the first part of Berger's book, I want also to pay fairly close attention to Fuller's commentary since he does not always represent Berger's argument fairly.

After his introductory section on seeing, Berger goes on to look at the way that when an image is presented as a work of art it is invariably mystified by assumptions concerning beauty, truth, genius and so on. As a specific example of this kind of mystification he quotes a passage from a discussion of two late paintings by Frans Hals in which Seymour Slive, a critic, speaks of 'harmonious fusion' and 'unforgettable contrast'. Berger then goes on to offer his own reading of the painting: for him the essential quality of the painting is the drama of the pauper Hals painting those on whose charity he depends. Here the authors of *Art-Language* have a point: 'Seymour Slive's book on Hals is the high bourgeois version; *Ways of Seeing*'s the petty bourgeois tear-jerking one.'⁷ Fuller's reservations about Berger's discussion of Slive and Hals is more elaborate. Here Fuller objects to the way that Berger 'appeals *convincingly* to the *authority of the paintings themselves*' after he (Berger) has claimed that it is exactly this authority which the means of technical reproduction have shattered.⁸

In fact, Berger does not refer to the authority of the paintings themselves but to the images reproduced. i.e. to photographed details of the original. This would be quibbling were it not for the fact that it is Fuller who makes the distinction, and his argument rests on it. Far from appealing to the authority of the original, Berger appeals to the new authority of the reproduced image. Fuller then goes on to say that Slive's account is not reducible to ideology but 'by treating it as such Berger comes close to throwing the baby out with the bath water.'⁹ Berger nowhere suggests that Slive's account *is* reducible to ideology though he *does* cite Slive as an example of the way that formalism *mystifies* rather than *clarifies*. Unless formalism is synonymous with ideology then Fuller himself is performing exactly the same feat of baby and bath water expulsion of which he accused Berger.

In similar style, Fuller comes up with his own version of Sartre's comment on Valéry: Berger is wrong to stress Hals's way of seeing rather than his way of *painting*, says Fuller, since many paupers in seventeenth-century Haarlem saw the governors as Hals did, but very few of them could have painted them as he did.¹⁰ 'This', says Fuller, 'is not a trivial or insubstantial quibble'. I think, however, that it *is*, since Berger has already introduced the Hals painting as 'great' and, in any case, his analysis is not intended to prove the painting's value but to show some of the elements of the painting tacitly shunted aside by Slive's formalism. What we are looking at is a way of seeing as revealed by, as *inscribed in*, a way of painting. (Fuller is right, on the other hand, to point to the contradiction between Berger's saying that we see the art of the past in a different way to people before us, and his more specific claim that we respond to the Hals because 'we still live in a society of comparable social relations and moral values'. Berger seems to be claiming that everything is the same and yet everything is different. Which is it to be?)

Fuller's criticism of Berger's analysis of the Hals paintings is, finally, that Berger 'lacks a fully materialist theory of expression' which is necessary for an understanding of the transforming work upon specific materials of a human subject. Since Berger's reason for discussing Hals's painting is to illustrate some of the mystifying procedures of bourgeois criticism, such a theory of expression is not essential to his purpose; but it is necessary for Fuller to make much of it in order to introduce the larger and more significant point that Berger does not distinguish adequately between a painting and a reproduction of it. In a photographic reproduction, Fuller remarks, 'the nature of the original is not wholly assimilated into the copy; nor can we regard the original, as Berger seems to do, as just a drained residue from which all that is of value, has been detached'.[11] Berger is thus guilty of 'a new kind of left idealism' where original paintings are reduced to their reproduced images – a point underlined, notes Fuller, by the poor quality of reproductions in the book.

Fuller later notes that he has no wish to travesty Berger's argument and that there are, in fact, a few parenthetical asides where Berger seems grudgingly to admit that paintings are not the same as photographs. The technique is not an unfamiliar one in criticism: to travesty someone else's argument and then acquit yourself of the doubts that are forming in the reader's mind by voicing those doubts yourself in the form of a denial. But Fuller's paraphrase *is* a travesty. In the first place the objection to the quality of the book's reproductions is ludicrous: how could Berger have 'juxtaposed his pin-up with the original', or, given the cost of quality reproduction, with 'a good reproduction of Ingres'?[12]

Secondly, Berger is emphatic that 'original paintings are silent and still in a sense that information never is'. The passage is emphatic but brief, at least partly because it is difficult for Berger to prove his case without, as it were, *reproducing the originals*. In the TV programmes, as Fuller was aware, where Berger had at least the advantage of colour, he went to some lengths to try to convey that silence. The camera holds for long, uninterrupted moments on Vermeers and Rembrandts; Berger attempts to articulate – without disturbing – their effect on us. An original painting, he explains, 'becomes a corridor connecting the moments it represents with the moments at which you are looking at it and something travels down that corridor at a speed greater than light, throwing into question our way of measuring time itself.' (Years later, in another television series, *About Time*, Berger managed a much more successful exposition of this effect in his comments on Rembrandt's *Woman in Bed*.) In the third programme of the series there is a powerful evocation of the peculiar silence of Vermeer's *Woman with Scales*: 'It is as though she's holding the moment between her forefinger and thumb on the scales of the past and the future. Despite its celebration of property, this painting is about the celebration of light and time as we look up at the stars'.

Painting as a celebration of private property – in particular the special relation that existed between property and oil painting between about 1500 and 1900 – is the central concern of the third part of the book *Ways of Seeing*. Berger's thesis can be stated simply: 'A way of seeing the world, which was ultimately determined by new attitudes towards property and exchange, found its visual expression in the oil painting, and could not have found it in any other visual art'. The reason for this was the unique ability of oil painting to convey 'a vision of total exteriority'. The subject matter of oil painting was almost always property, and the oil painting itself was, and still is, primarily an object, a piece of property that lets the owner of the painting 'possess' what was depicted in the painting. In stressing the 'tangibility' of the objects in oil painting, Berger was proceeding from what had for some time been the uncontested starting point for discussion: Bernard Berenson's 'tactile values'. The early Florentine painters, said Berenson, convey in their paintings 'a keener sense of reality, of lifelikeness, than the objects themselves'. The painter aims to give 'an abiding sense impression of artistic reality with only two dimensions', and this can only be done 'by giving tactile values to retinal impressions'. 'His first business therefore,' Berenson goes on, 'is to rouse the tactile sense, for I must have the illusion of being able to touch a figure.'[13]

Berger himself quotes Berenson in the essay 'Past Seen from a Possible Future' and takes him literally at his word: oil painting enables us not simply to touch but to take possession.

> European means of representation refer to the experience of taking possession. Just as its perspective gathers all that is extended to render it to the individual eye, so its means of representation render all that is depicted into the hands of the individual owner-spectator. Painting becomes the metaphorical act of appropriation. (*L.T.* p.215)

The essay begins with Berger wondering just how many oil paintings have actually been produced; from there it is a short step to realizing what will be a central and memorable claim of *Ways of Seeing*: that only a tiny fraction of the paintings actually produced can be considered as serious works of art. Art history tries to pass off this fraction as the only history worth considering, ignoring the nine-tenths of the iceberg deceptively submerged beneath the surface of quality. However, by attending to what Anthony Barnett later called 'the totality of the average',[14] we are furnished with the most explicit evidence of the real concerns of European oil painting; with evidence, in Berger's words, 'of the way that the European ruling classes saw the world and themselves'.[15]

No one, as Fuller rightly observes, has ever refuted Berger's analysis of the relation of oil painting to private property; he 'may therefore be said to have delivered an historic blow to the self-conception of 'civilized' man'.

Our reservations about Berger's argument are his own, namely that Berger's survey of the traditional oil painting has been 'very brief and therefore very crude'.[16] In such a survey, exceptions to the general thesis are glossed over and, more importantly, the relationship between art and property is assumed to be – or rather, is left as – a straightforward and relatively constant one. The relation between property, patrons and the means of figuration is taken as stable rather than as complex, dynamic and shifting – actively creating the effective variation and *development* of paintings of property.[17] While Berger suggests an equation between art and property, the relationship is better seen as a larger matrix of social forces. In place of an investigation of the historical specificity of the relation of oil painting and property, whose nature – since what we are really concerned with here is a metaphor and expression of power – itself changes over the period with which Berger is concerned, Berger picks a number of particular examples to illustrate a general theory. Holbein's *The Ambassadors* and Gainsborough's *Mr and Mrs Andrews* may well both be celebrations of private property but they are very different paintings. By leaving the relationship between art and property as constant, this variation can only be explained in the formalist or idealist terms that Berger opposes. While there is no need to reproach Berger for leaving to others the task of a more detailed examination of the relationship between art and property at a given historical moment or within a particular genre, this lack is closely related to what Berger later described as 'the immense theoretical weakness' of his book.

At the end of the chapter, Berger comes back to the exceptional painters who 'broke free of the norms of the tradition'. Far from being the supreme representatives of the tradition, writes Berger, these artists, in their great works, were involved in an active struggle to produce work 'that was diametrically opposed to its values'. On several occasions, Berger has written scathingly of the myth of the struggling artist but by speaking of the exceptional artist as if s/he is, by definition, in opposition to his/her situation, Berger comes close to creating his own version of the same myth. He ends the chapter by contrasting Rembrandt's exuberant, early and unexceptional portrait of himself and his beloved Saskia with a later exceptional portrait of himself in a state of emotional destitution. Contrary to the conventions of oil painting, this self-portrait broods with 'a sense of the question of existence, of existence as a question'.

Berger makes no mention of the great paintings which were produced not against the current of tradition but at – and as a result of – the confluence of historical and art historical forces. Some of David's greatest paintings, for example, are the products of being buoyed along by the sweep of historical events as they coincided with the artistic means available to him.

In the commentary to the series Berger speaks of how, intermittently, 'the tradition can breed within itself a counter-tradition'. This mitigates the claims of the book but the point is left undeveloped. What is clear is that the relationship between 'exceptional' and 'normative' changes and can only be understood within a particular art-historical context. By leaving the relationship between property and painting as a constant, Berger is left with only one motor or lever of change: the 'exceptional' artist whose relation with the normative tradition is also constant – and so we are back into the realm of the transhistorical and idealist.

That Berger was aware of a problem here is made clear in the article 'In Defence of Art' (reprinted in *The White Bird* as 'The *Work* of Art') when he wrote that 'the immense theoretical weakness' of *Ways of Seeing* 'is that I do not make clear what relation exists between what I call "the exception" (the genius) and the normative tradition. It is at this point that work needs to be done'. This later comment is still 'tainted' by the legacy of the earlier problem. As Peter Fuller rightly notes, the distinction between the exceptional and the normative is 'over-sharp' and 'too dualistic', ignoring the real gradation of value that exists between these poles. We will return to this preoccupation of Berger's later.

Germaine Greer's *The Female Eunuch* was published in Britain in 1970, and *Women's Estate* by Juliet Mitchell in 1971. The word 'patriarchy', in its currently accepted general sense of the domination of society by men, only became widely known with the publication in 1970 of Kate Millett's *Sexual Politics*. Berger's *Ways of Seeing* came out during this first wave of the new feminist movement. Since then a voluminous literature on representations of women has developed. At the time (witness the discussion in the TV series of the issues raised), Berger's consideration of the history of the female nude was a breakthrough.

The main ideas for the discussion of the nude in *Ways of Seeing* were sketched out in the seminal essay of 1970, 'Past Seen From a Possible Future', which itself drew on suggestions and observations from Berger's writings on art from the previous 15 years. Once again, though, the intentions of *Ways of Seeing* define themselves most clearly in opposition to Kenneth Clark, whose book, *The Nude: A Study in Ideal Form* (1956) was, and for many still is, the standard work on the subject. 'To be naked', announced Clark, 'is to be deprived of our clothes'; the nude, on the other hand, brings to mind an image 'not of a huddled and defenceless body, but of a balanced, prosperous and confident body: the body reformed'. The nude, then, is not 'the subject of art, but a form of art'.[18]

Clark admits that 'it is necessary to labour the obvious and say that no nude, however abstract, should fail to arouse in the spectator some vestige of erotic feeling . . . and if it does not do so, it is bad art and false morals'.[19] For all the manly frankness of this pronouncement, and for all its scholarly impressiveness, what follows is an essay remarkable both in its euphemism and in its oddly salacious idealism. Although Clark's is a book about the male and female nude, it is only in discussing the latter that he is at all troubled by notions of eroticism. The male nude is dealt with in masculine terms of vigour, strength and power, unembarrassed by any hint of lasciviousness.[20] The discussion of the female nude, on the other hand, is saturated with the language of titillation and arousal to such an extent that the combination of cool connoisseurship and sensual delectation can be seen as symptomatic of the whole tradition of male production and discussion of images of women. Thus one of the women in Giorgione's *Concert Champêtre* is 'painted with an unprejudiced sensuality as if she were a peach or a pear'.[21] The most vivid example of Clark's 'innocent disingenuousness' is probably his discussion of Boucher's extraordinarily rude painting, *Miss O'Murphy*. Miss O'Murphy is lying on her stomach on a dishevelled couch. Her legs are wide open, cushions and linen are bunched suggestively between her legs. In its flagrant naughtiness Boucher's image is one of the great what-the-butler-saw masterpieces in painting, but for Clark it shows Boucher as 'an eager and perceptive admirer of the body'. 'By art Boucher has enabled us to enjoy her with as little shame as she is enjoying herself. One false note and we should be embarrassingly back in the world of sin'.[22] One *false* note indeed! Clark's account, for all its personal whims, is essentially a history of what Gombrich called 'schemata' – the formal conventions that enabled artists to generalize from the particular. What for Clark is a means of diffusing the explicit content of a picture is, for Berger, simply anonymity. While agreeing with Clark that the nude is a 'special' category, Berger purposes a radical redefinition of naked and nude. 'To be naked is to be oneself. To be nude is to be seen naked by others and yet not recognized for oneself. A naked body has to be seen as an object in order to become a nude ... nakedness reveals itself. Nudity is placed on display' (*W.S.* p.54). The nude is dressed in the clothes of the 'owner-spectator's' expectations and desires. She is condemned to never being naked, to feed appetites but have none of her own. Most of the nudes in the European tradition of oil are no more than the sum of their conventions:

> I am in front of a typical European nude. She is painted with extreme sensuous emphasis. Yet her sexuality is only superficially manifest in her actions or her own expression; in a comparable figure within other art traditions this would not be so. Why? Because for Europe ownership is primary. The painting's sexuality is manifest not in what it shows but in the owner-spectator's (mine in this case) right to see her naked. Her nakedness is not a function of her sexuality but of the sexuality of those who have access to the picture. In the majority of European nudes there is a close parallel with the passivity which is endemic to prostitution. (*L.T.* p.215)

In their unambiguous appeal to 'the man looking at the picture', there is much in common between an Ingres nude and an image from a soft-porn magazine. Similarly in that favourite subject of painters, 'The Judgement of Paris', there are precise parallels with the beauty contests of today. However, reservation must be expressed here. Juxtaposition can become dangerously ahistorical;

an image from *Playboy* may bear a striking resemblance to a Boucher or an Ingres, but it is also very different, not, as Fuller claims, because painting takes more effort than photography but because of the intervening history. The meaning of an image does not reside only in what is depicted and how it is depicted. The meaning of a pin-up is inseparable from its deliberate and conscious response to, and exploitation of, the opportunities and deprivations created by the conditions of modernity: mass reproduction and distribution, changes in sexual morality and the status of women, and the 'uses' to which sexuality is put. This is implicit in the central thesis of *Ways of Seeing*, that mass reproduction changes the nature of the image; it is explicit in Berger's essay 'Goya: The Maja, Dressed and Undressed'. In that essay, Berger claims that Goya's painting of the Maja Undressed is shockingly prophetic, anticipating 'the aestheticism of sex' which, in the second half of the twentieth century, 'helps to keep a consumer society stimulated, competitive and dissatisfied'.[23] A pin-up is part of this aestheticism of sex; the Ingres painting was produced in an entirely different context, before the phenomenon of the aestheticism of sex existed. Thus, to see pin-ups as mass reproductions of Ingres nudes is to beg the question, to gloss over the history contained in the fact of mass reproduction.

Berger's discussion of the female nude is argued in the context of a consideration of 'the social presence of women', developed from ideas being worked out in the process of writing *G*. (Many passages in *G* are identical to those in *Ways of Seeing*.) A man's presence, says Berger, has always suggested what he is capable of doing; a woman's presence suggests 'what can and what cannot be done to her'. 'One might simplify this by saying: men act and women appear. Men look at women. Women watch themselves being looked at'. This constant self-scrutiny could easily be derided by men as an indication of women's vanity, providing male artists with an artistic 'device' which has not fallen out of favour for 400 years: 'You painted a naked woman because you enjoyed looking at her, you put a mirror in her hand and you called the painting *Vanity*, thus morally condemning the woman whose nakedness you had depicted for your own pleasure' (*W.S.* p.51).

As in the tradition of paintings of property there are, among the thousands of conventional nudes, 'perhaps a hundred' that break the norms of convention: 'they are paintings of loved women, more or less naked. . . In each case the painter's personal vision of the particular woman he is painting is so strong that it makes no allowance for the spectator'. Berger's explanation is true of the paintings he cites – a Rembrandt, a Rubens – but the transforming power of love is an inadequate general explanation of the 'exceptional' nude: in fact it is not really an explanation but a plea for exemption – and such a plea, as Berger later remarked, is always at the heart of sentimentality. One of the very greatest painters and drawers of the female nude, Egon Schiele, gives the lie to Berger's claim, most obviously in his 1910 sketch 'Self portrait drawing a nude model in front of a mirror'. It would be disingenuous to claim that Schiele's pictures are about love. They are about sex, voyeurism, arousal, staring. Almost all his nudes are depicted with the same burning sexual intensity – so much so that there is, in a way, no difference between a Schiele painting of a nude and a self portrait. Many of Schiele's best nudes are, in a sense, portraits of himself masturbating (and some of Schiele's paintings are called exactly that).

Schiele's peculiar example points to a larger weakness in Berger's method. This method is neither inductive nor deductive. He moves between the general and the particular to formulate a thesis that can serve as an authentic 'caption' for all the evidence with which he is concerned. While this implies thorough formulation, it does not enable Berger to move from fairly comprehensive annotation to a systematic examination of representations of the female nude. Commenting on the 'average' nude, Berger stresses that the paintings were made for a male owner-spectator and that the passivity of the depicted women is a response to his needs. Linda Nochlin, however, has pointed out that such passivity is a function not only of the owner-spectator but also of the artist-creator, as in the myth of Pygmalion.[24] The only time that Berger considers the artist's intentions is when he is discussing the exceptional nude. On these occasions, as Lynda Nead points out: 'meaning is seen to be a product of the painter's individual feelings and experiences and the image is thus removed from its place in the process of reproduction of male domination over women.'[25]

Rather than being seen as illustrations of the power of the owner-spectator or as expressions of the individual artists, images of women need to be seen as 'the actual site of production' of male domination of women, as agents of manufacture. The individual artist is not likely to be able to exempt himself from the sexual ideologies of his time as they are inscribed in a visual system *simply* by the special nature of his relationship with a loved model. As Griselda Pollock has put it:

> The individual artist does not simply express himself but is rather the privileged user of the language of his culture which pre-exists him as a series of historically reinforced codes, signs and meanings which he manipulates or even transforms but can never exist outside of.[26]

Since 1972, more attention has been devoted to unravelling this system of 'codes, signs and meanings' than to the specific intentions and effects of a particular artist or painting. Berger quality-tests paintings of the nude against a particular version of the real – the nude as beloved. The unexceptional painting is seen as an anonymous version of an individual, a falling short of the real. Berger does not consider that any idea of the real is 'constituted through the agency of representations'.[27] Although, as noted, Berger's consideration of the nude is developed in the context of a discussion of the social presence of women, the images analyzed are seen as 'reflections' or proof of the domination of women by men; they are never considered as an active part in the production of that reality to which they refer. It is not a question of owner-spectator or artist-creator, or even, as in a few exceptional paintings, of artist-lover, but of the complex interaction of a system of communication in which representations of women simultaneously reflect, perpetuate, transform and create a patriarchal reality.

Having said that, we must end this chapter on the same note as it began and emphasize again that it was *Ways of Seeing*, more than any other single text at the time, that initiated this debate and opened it to a wide audience.

10. *A Seventh Man* and *Another Way of Telling*

Some there are who live in darkness
While the others live in light
We see those who live in daylight
Those in darkness, out of sight.
Berthold Brecht

A Seventh Man continues the project of *Ways of Seeing* in attempting to use the reproduced image to radicalize rather than to glamourize, to authenticate rather than to seduce. It is also Berger's most fiercely political book, an urgent, unsentimental account of the degradation on which European prosperity depends. In its explicit commitment to the belief that the true meaning of power is best measured by those who live most powerlessly under it, in its attempt to come to terms with the inarticulate truth hidden from the eyes of the relatively privileged, it looks forward to Berger's later work in *Pig Earth*, to the photographic project of *Another Way of Telling*, and to the meditation on exile in *And Our Faces*.

In confining myself to a few remarks about Berger's language and method in *A Seventh Man*, I am not seeking to 'reduce' it to a work of literature and thereby shield myself from the reality to which it refers. Exactly the opposite: the point is that more than any other work of Berger's it speaks for itself. Each paragraph announces itself unequivocally: 'To be homeless is to be nameless. He. The existence of a migrant worker.' Although Berger analyses in detail the world economic system that depends on migrant labour, he is wary of the way 'statistics tend to distract', making us 'consider numbers instead of pain'. The language of economic theory is 'too abstract and a less abstract formulation is needed': metaphor.

Metaphor and theory, the novelistic and the documentary, are concentrated into the simple pronoun 'he' (Berger is concerned exclusively with male migrant workers). 'He' is the representative *in extremis* of all migrant workers (his sensations are metaphors for everyone else's) and the point of convergence of economic forces in history. Through him, the abstract becomes real. His own actual experiences are soaked in theory in the way that a sponge is soaked in water, containing and shaping one another:

> For the rest of the evening in the barracks 'he' wears something he wore at home – a robe, a coloured shirt, sandals with bare feet, a skullcap, perhaps a woollen shawl. In its folds, or texture, or the way it fits him, there is a residue from the past, and this acts as a kind of physical insulation against the present. (*S.M.* p. 188)

Metaphor becomes a description of sensation and a theory of the origins of that sensation.

> The prisoner suffers the double pain of absence. He misses everything he feels as absent. At the same time, that which is absent continues without him. He lacks and is lacking. Yet absence is not final loss. His sentence has an end. He can envisage how he will rejoin the absent. This is a source of hope but it is also the pivot of the violence of imprisonment. Increasingly he may begin to live by way of memory and anticipation, until the two of them become indistinguishable, until he anticipates his release in the future as the moment when he will rejoin all that was left in the past. Imprisonment is designed as the categorical denial of the present (*S.M.* p. 178)

It is as if – and here I am only concerned to describe an effect – the argument has been lived through and not simply reasoned out, as if the argument can be refuted only by greater fidelity to lived experience. (Thought for Berger, as many of those who have met him will confirm, is almost a form of physical exertion.)

A comparison with Naipaul. Here is a passage from 'Tell Me Who To Kill' in *In a Free State*:

> I work and work and save and save and the money grow and grow, and when it reach two thousand pounds, I get stunned. I don't feel I can go on. I know the life have to stop sometime, that I can't go on with two jobs, that something have to happen.

And now the thought of working and saving another thousand is too much for me. . .

The money make me feel strong. The money make me feel that money is easy. The money make me forget how hard money is to make, that it take me four years to save what I have. The money is in my hand, two thousand pounds, make me forget that my father never got more than ten pounds a month for his donkey-cart work, that he bring all of us up on that ten pounds a month, and that ten by twelve is one hundred and twenty, that the money I have in my hand is the pay of my father for fifteen or sixteen years.[1]

Naipaul's narrator is a West Indian migrant who moves through the same stages of experience that are noticed by Berger. Unlike Berger, Naipaul never makes explicit the forces at work on his narrator's life; they are constantly felt but never directly manifested, part of the fabric of the migrant's consciousness. Berger all the time comments omnisciently on what the migrant is living through: 'through his own individual effort he tries to achieve the dynamism that is lacking in the situation in which he finds himself' (the characteristic circumstance and ethic of a typical Naipaul character). Naipaul has great sensitivity to the rhythms and richness of West Indian speech; like Naipaul, Berger conveys the authentic voice of the migrant, 'the sound of the unknown language', but the idiom is less specific. The similies and the rhythm of the prose duplicate the migrant's efforts to understand what happens to him in terms of the only point of reference he has: the village. Liquid leaks out of a machine 'like liquid that gathers round a fish's mouth when it has been taken out of the water and has stopped thrashing'. But Berger does not stop there. The passage continues: 'He knows that what he is doing is separate from any skill he has. He can stuff a saddle with straw. He has been told that the factory makes washing machines.'[2]

Although it deals with displacement and loss, the recognizable origins of the narrator's language in Naipaul's writing irresistibly suggest the distant but specific home that he misses. Berger's rhythm is less rooted in a specific place; it lacks exactly that sense of specific origin which is so powerful in Naipaul's work. It is a shadow language, a language of alienation that is at home nowhere. Later, in *And Our Faces*, Berger writes that language is perhaps the last human refuge, 'the only dwelling place that cannot be hostile to man'.[3] In *A Seventh Man*, that refuge is at its most feeble; its language is the voice of homelessness.

The disembodied quality of Berger's language is not simply a question of third person as opposed to first person narration, nor is it a question of moving in and out of the migrant's consciousness. Rather, the rhythms and images of the migrant combine with Berger's familiar 'secularized millenial' narrative mode to produce an absence and a tenderness, a language that is both anonymous and personal. Berger's simple claim – 'To be homeless is to be nameless, He, the existence of a migrant worker' – is thus inscribed in the whole conception and method of the book.

In *A Seventh Man*, the collaboration with photographer Jean Mohr is more complete than in *A Fortunate Man*; the photographs play a more active part. Many of the migrants cannot speak for themselves in the way that Sassall could. Berger speaks for them, but Mohr records their silence. He captures what Berger can only describe as the 'in-turned look' which many have. Above all, the photographs convey concretely the unique anonymity of the migrant worker. This provides documentary proof – an anchoring in the particular – of what Berger is attempting in his prose.

With Berger's text the photographs succeed in achieving an almost impossible reciprocity: the migrants are as we see them and they are not as we see them; this is how we see the migrants and this is *not how they see themselves but how they feel themselves being seen*. Take the photograph 'Migrants and others watching civic fete, Avignon, France' (pp.198-9). The proximity of the migrants to the Europeans enhances their separation from them. The stare of the three migrants: they look different to everyone else and they are *looking differently*. 'The histories of the last two centuries is nothing less than infernal.' It has taken that history to produce that look. There is perhaps a superficial resemblance in their stare to that of the walkers in Edvard Munch's painting *Evening on Karl Johan's Street* (1893) but the effect is very different. Munch's paranoid gawping is projected onto the passers by. The photo does not simply record our impression of the scene, our version of the migrants' look: their look is their own. It is not a photo about *how* migrants look (appear), as is the case with much social documentary, but the *way* they look (see).

For a more detailed analysis of Berger and Mohr's way of working, we can turn to the sequence of photographs surrounding the central image of three migrants in a room plastered with pornographic pictures of women (pp. 172-5). Berger and Mohr wanted to use the photo as an 'indirect index of the sexual deprivation suffered by these men' but the problem was how to use it without appearing either to approve of the 'virulent sexism' of the images or to reduce it to simple evidence of the migrants' misogyny. They tried several alternatives but in the end decided to add two pictures before and one after so as to form a sequence. The first is of an old peasant woman who could have been the mother of one of these migrants; it is 'the kind of picture that one of those workers might have carried round with him'. Next to this they put a Madonna by Perugino so that there begins to be 'a juxtaposition between ideal-ized maternity and real maternity'. Then comes the picture of the men surrounded by images of women. We are 'beginning to relate, to talk about a life story, beginning to talk about women in more than one dimension, beginning to talk about the experience of those men'. The final photo in the sequence is of a young peasant girl. It is the exact opposite of the photos on the wall and probably closely resembles one of the girls in the migrants' own village. The sequence as a whole provides a context and a deeper meaning to the initial image of the men in the barracks.[4]

Berger and Mohr work separately at first. 'I never have the feel-ing of having to take pictures to illustrate the text or John having to write the captions and text to make a point about my pictures', says Mohr.[5] After the project's inception, at the initial stage, they do not see each other's work; later, they work together to pull everything into coherent shape. Their collaborative project is taken to its logical extreme in *Another Way of Telling*. Published in 1982 it complements and is intimately connected with Berger's work in *Pig Earth* but is more conveniently dealt with here. The heart of the book is a sequence of 150 captionless pictures evoking the story of a peasant woman's life which attempts to construct 'a truly photographic narrative form'. It does not attempt to tell, in the sense of document, the woman's life but to use the language of appearances 'so as not only to illustrate, but also to articulate a lived experience'.[6]

The difficulty of constructing such a sequence stems from the inherent nature of the photograph, which Berger discusses not only in *Another Way of Telling* but also in essays such as 'Under-standing a Photograph' and 'Uses of Photography'. Unlike a drawing, which contains the time of its own making, the photo, says Berger, 'arrests the flow of time', 'isolates the appearance of a disconnected instant'. Drawing on Susan Sontag's notion of

photos as 'a trace, something directly stencilled off from the real',
Berger argues that photographs 'do not translate from appearances' but, instead, *quote* from them. Thus photographs are 'irre-
futable as evidence but weak in meaning.'[7] This is because
meaning is not instantaneous: 'Meaning is discovered in what con-
nects and cannot exist without development. Without a story,
without an unfolding, there is no meaning.'[8]

After an analysis of André Kertesz's photograph of 'A Red
Hussar Leaving, June 1919, Budapest' Berger goes on to claim that
the exceptional individual photo is expressive because of the
'quality' of the quotation, because of its 'narrative range'. The expressive photograph, in other words, quotes from reality at greater
length, though this length should be measured not in terms of an
extension in time but in meaning: 'It is not time that is prolonged,
but meaning.'[9]

The sequence of photographs called 'If Each Time. . .' attempts
to turn isolated quotations into a story. While photographs isolate, Berger and Mohr are attempting to 'un-isolate',[10] to give a
sense of unfolding that is not dependent on linear narrative.
Photographs so organized 'are restored to a living context': 'the
world they reveal, frozen becomes tractable. The information
they contain becomes permeated by feeling. Appearances become
the language of a lived life.'[11]

This is lucid commentary but there is a sense in which its very
lucidity undermines the ambitions of the photographic sequence
which it accompanies. It is an admission that the wordless sequence of photographs cannot convey what is intended without
being bracketed between verbal explanations from Berger. The
photographs do not work as another way of *telling*, as a storytelling *sequence* because, as Anthony Barnett suggested to me,
they are unable to sustain a narrative (though, of course, the meaning of each image is altered by its relationship to those that surround it). Rather, the photographs are a form of visual *poetry*.
This is not a comment on the inadequacy of Berger and Mohr's
undertaking, but on the current state of the visual grammar of
photography.

'If Each Time. . .' is concerned with forging a visual grammar
and as a whole *Another Way of Telling* fulfills what Berger sees as
one of the tasks of a photographic project opposed to the dominant uses of the image. Such an alternative depends on the
photographer 'thinking of her or himself not so much as a reporter
to the rest of the world but, rather, as a recorder for the events

photographed'. Mohr's photographs have always been marked by a sense of unobtrusiveness. We are scarcely aware of the photographer taking them. It is as if the photographs are not taken by Mohr but given by his subjects. Mohr has himself commented on this delicacy towards his subjects during the work on *A Fortunate Man*:

> There were some moments where I didn't want to take pictures but it was the doctor who reminded me of my duty . . . for instance, one little story which appears in the book is of an old couple. The wife was depressed, she had a breakdown, and they came in the middle of the afternoon, both on a motorcycle or side car. She was in the middle of her forties and he was completely lost. Probably the breakdown had to do with her age. They had lived together for more than 20 or 25 years and he was just completely lost. He brought her to the doctor and she was crying and he was lost and I felt at that moment that it was too private and I didn't want to take pictures but the doctor reminded me and said: 'If you want to show what is the life of a doctor, this belongs also to my practice. I don't have only to cure physical things.' Which was true.[12]

The photographs in *Another Way of Telling* are even more straightforwardly for the benefit of those photographed. The photos of Gaston, the woodcutter, were 'made' at the request of his wife: 'Would you take a photo of my husband? I don't have one, and if he's killed in the forest I won't have a picture to remember him by'. Gaston agrees to the photos being taken on condition that they 'show what the *work* is like'. When he sees the pictures he exclaims: 'That's the photo I dreamt of since I began cutting down trees.'[13] When Marcel, the herdsman, saw Mohr's portrait he said, 'with a kind of relief: "And now my great grandchildren will know what sort of man I was." '[14]

11. *Pig Earth*

I've gathered these voices without shaking loose the dust of the earth from which they spring.
Danilo Dolci

Since 1974, Berger has lived in a small peasant community in Haute Savoie, France. In 1979 he published *Pig Earth*, a volume of essays, poems and stories set in that area. The book is the first volume of a proposed trilogy concerned with 'the intricate movement from peasant society to metropolis'. Recognizing this movement as fundamental to the foundation of modernity, the trilogy 'Into Their Labours' is a hugely ambitious project, following from his earlier work on migrant labour in *A Seventh Man* and marked by a similar commitment to those whose lives are buried beneath European prosperity.

At the time of writing, the second volume of the trilogy is almost complete. Having read most of the second volume in manuscript, I think it is likely that in the next century 'Into Their Labours' will come to be regarded as one of Berger's major achievements and one of the most important works of our time. Here I will concern myself only with *Pig Earth*.

In *Pig Earth* the peasant struggles to exist; Berger struggles to give 'a meaning to experience'. He conceives of this struggle as the labour of the storyteller, a labour which seems now – the retrospective vision has its own distortions: projecting a fixity of purpose onto the screen of the past – to represent the fulfilment of his earliest ambitions: 'I often think that even when I was writing on art, it was really a way of telling stories'.[1] Berger saw Sassall as part of a vocational tradition that reached back to Paracelsus; the tradition of storytellers of which Berger sees himself as being a part reaches back to those 'who first invented and then named the constellations'. In his own time, Berger enters a democratic fraternity of kindred spirits. 'In some countries critics have compared my own recent fiction with [Garcia Marquez] and it is true that I see

him, not as a critic but as a colleague in an art of storytelling.'[2]
Talking with a 'hard, indefatigable, 70-year-old cattle raiser' Berger noticed

> an expression in his eyes, a certain look of complicity. About what? About something we share despite the obvious differences. . . For a long time I puzzled over this. And suddenly I realized what it was. It was his recognition of our equal intelligence; we are both historians of our time. We both see how events fit together. . . The expression I caught in his eyes was both bright and consoling. It was the look of one storyteller to another. (*W.B.* p. 14)

Berger's conception of himself as storyteller owes, as we shall see, a great deal to Walter Benjamin's essay of that name. 'Experience which is passed on from mouth to mouth,' comments Benjamin, 'is the source from which all storytellers have drawn'.[3] Berger's stories have their origin in those that the village tells about itself – stories of the past and the immediate present. These stories begin as gossip and become history so that the village produces 'a living portrait of itself'; they are narrated neither 'to idealize [n]or condemn; rather they testify to the always slightly surprising range of the possible'.[4] They are an 'organic part of the life of the village' and to tell them Berger has to be a part of that community. At the same time that he is a part of the community he is also separate from it; his position as a writer is both link and barrier, he is both 'witness and stranger': 'The act of approaching a given moment of experience involves both scrutiny (closeness) and the capacity to connect (distance).'[5] Benjamin comments on exactly this dual perspective:

> When someone goes on a trip, he has something to tell about, goes the German saying, and people imagine the storyteller as someone who has come from afar. But they enjoy no less listening to the man who has stayed at home, making an honest living, and who knows the local tales and traditions. If one wants to picture these two groups through their archaic representatives, one is embodied in the resident tiller of the soil, and the other in the trading seaman.

Benjamin goes on to point out that the 'actual extension of the realm of storytelling in its full historical breadth is inconceivable without the most intimate interpenetration of these two archaic types'. Berger's own attempt to attain this 'full corporeality' of the storyteller is seen in its most developed form in 'The Three Lives of Lucy Cabrol'. The narrator of the story is born and grows up in the same village as Lucy Cabrol but emigrates and spends 25 years in Argentina and then some time in Canada. When he returns to the village after these years in exile, his perspective is both that of the tiller and the seaman.

Since the time of the romantics the idealization of simple, rural life has been a staple of our culture. For the romantics the encounter with the natural man was essentially a chance meeting with a stranger in the middle of nowhere; but the terms of the meeting, the discursive terrain, are almost always determined by the writer/poet. The most obvious example is 'Resolution and Independence' where Wordsworth asks the leech-gatherer about his philosophy of life but is so spellbound by the meeting that he forgets to listen. It is a fleeting encounter with a being 'from another world', full of all sorts of significances which Wordsworth will puzzle out later. When he is not getting philosophical value for money out of his meetings, Wordsworth becomes impatient: 'A while on trivial things we held discourse/To me soon tasteless' ('The Ruined Cottage'). Berger's ambitions are the opposite of Wordsworthian. The stories in the village where Berger lives are told by people who are known to each other. Berger can only do justice to these stories by telling them on their own terms. This does not mean simply repeating them. It means conceiving and writing *Pig Earth* as something very different to a novel. Benjamin the storyteller takes what he tells from experience – his own or that reported by others. And he in turn makes it the experience of those who are listening to his tale. The novelist has isolated himself. Drawing on Benjamin's distinction, Berger sees the chronicle as something which 'retells more memorably what is already generally known',[6] while the novel reveals what is private. The peasant's memory elides past and present events; and while in a novel events unfold in a causal sequence the chronicle allows past and present to coexist.

The terms of Berger's stories, then, are almost the opposite of the typically romantic encounter. As Van Gogh tries to make his paintings *be* what they represent so Berger's writing aspires to the condition of perfect listening. (Recording is passive; perfect listening is active.) The main body of the book is uncharacteristically self-effacing, untypically free of the sense of Berger's dominating creative personality. This is most obviously true at the level of style. This explains, I think, why, on re-reading *Pig Earth*, I was struck by the way I had forgotten what a good book it is. We are used to the most impressive similes being the most startling and spectacular. Here there is a fresh *familiarity* about them: 'Four times the birth had released a flow of milk into her immense udder which was like a full moon coming up behind a hill'. 'His brows, his temples, the bridge of his nose were wrinkled like the skin of baked milk'. 'The sky was clear, the Milky Way like a vast misty white goose pecking at the lip of a jug.' 'His voice creaked like a pine tree in a storm.' 'In the east the snow on the mountains was turning a very diluted rose, no redder than the water of a stream when an animal has been killed.'[7]

The particular qualities of the language in *Pig Earth* can be brought out by a comparison. In the same year that Berger published the first volume of his trilogy, Ted Hughes published *Moortown*, the central sequence of which is a 'verse journal' recording his experiences farming in Devon. Many of the same events are depicted in both *Pig Earth* and *Moortown*; Hughes's understanding of animals and his feel for landscape are as intimate as and more longstanding than Berger's. Like Berger's, Hughes's is a book by someone who has not just observed but has worked with animals and land. His language is raw, violent, savagely matter-of-fact:

The needle between the horn and the eye, so deep
Your gut squirms for the eyeball twisting
In its pink-white fastening of tissue. This side and that.
Then the first one anaesthetized, back in the crush.
The bulldog pincers in the septum, stretched full strength,
The horn levered right over, the chin pulled round
With the pincers, the mouth drooling, the eye
Like a live eye caught in a pan, like the eye of a fish
Imprisoned in air. Then the cheese cutter
Of braided wire, and stainless steel peg handles,
Aligned on the hair-bedded root of the horn, then leaning
Backward full weight, pull-punching backwards,
Left right left right and the blood leaks
Down over the cheekbone. . .[8]

Here is a gentler passage – written at *the same level of intensity*:

Wind out of freezing Europe. A mean snow
Fiery cold. Ewes caked crusty with snow,
Their new hot lambs wet trembling
And crying on trampled patches, under the hedge –
Twenty miles of open lower landscape
Blows into their wetness.[9]

Hughes's language tends to the *excruciating*; it conveys action as *effects*. The language of *Pig Earth* conserves its energy without being parsimonious. It is not energetic writing but it is tireless, aware all the time of the demands that it makes on itself. There is not a single wasted word, and as such the book represents the perfection of effort. Berger's language is similar to the peculiar rhythm of peasants who walk 'as if testing the earth with each stride'. Like the peasants described in 'The Suit and the Photograph' his language possesses a 'a special physical dignity' which is 'determined by a kind of functionalism, a way of being *fully at home in effort*'.[10] In the last story of *Pig Earth*, Berger mentions the scythe that Lucy Cabrol never allows anyone else to use. 'Only the work of twenty summers can make a scythe as light as this', she says.[11] The language of *Pig Earth* has some of the qualities of that scythe: a sharpness and ease borne of active use.

The overall effects of the stories are inseparable from these qualities of language. In 1975, Berger reviewed a collection of stories from Sicily and noted that the short story is 'about a moment of truth'. He explains and quotes three such moments from the collection he is reviewing. This is one of them:

> A peasant made jealous of his wife, kills his small son with a hoe because he now believes he is not the father: '. . . in the vast field stretching in the sunshine, on the roads, along the winding paths, amidst the fresh green of the corn, not a living soul was to be seen. Only his donkey was staring at him, head erect and ears pricked, chewing a mouthful of straw under a sheltering roof by a cactus hedge.'[12]

The similarity of this kind of moment to some passages in *Pig Earth* is striking. In 'Lucy Cabrol' two maquisards arrive at the Cabrol farm. They are being hunted by the Germans:

> One of the two unknown men started down the slope. Half way, he emerged from the shadow of the mountain and entered

the early morning sunshine. He was short and burly and
walked like a peasant.

The two brothers stood absolutely still lest any movement be
interpreted by the stranger as a welcome. When he was a few
metres away, the stranger said, Good morning.

In the fields deliberate silence is a powerful weapon. Henri
said nothing, and withdrew his head back into his shoulders
like a dog guarding a doorway. Edmond stood with his hands
on his hips, staring insolently. (*P.E.* p.125)

Such moments are neither isolated nor climactic; they merge into
the general movements of events. To make them 'momentous' in
any way would be to re-insert the prerogatives of a narrative form
that is inappropriate to the lives depicted. In much Anglo-
American writing the 'key' moment involves a glimpse of that
which is illicit or hidden. The 'truth' revealed in such a moment is
either the opposite of what appeared to be the case or it serves to
reverse the assumptions held up to that point. In *Pig Earth* instead
of revelation there is a steadily growing familiarity; instead of the
resolution of uncertainties and contradictions there is an abiding
in them. There is no privileged information; many things remain
unknown, the identity of Lucy Cabrol's killer, for example. Berger refuses omniscience over his characters. There is no conspiracy
between author and reader, no irony. 'The art of the short story is
so to place the moment in the life or lives of which it is a part, that it
becomes impossible to judge it from the outside.'[13] Characteristically, the narrator of 'Lucy Cabrol' explains throughout the story
how he came by the information he is now recording and it becomes steadily more difficult to tell Lucy's story without telling
his own. He is unable to 'solve' the riddle of Lucy's murder and
'when the distinction between imagination and reality is effaced'
in the beautiful and 'uncanny' barn-building scene he becomes the
active representative of the reader's own uncertainty.[14] The movement of the book is towards a gradual immersion in the lives depicted. The effect is described in *Another Way of Telling*: 'You were
listening. You were in the story. You were in the words of the
storyteller. You were no longer your single self; you were, thanks
to the story, everyone it concerned.'[15] Benjamin similarly notes
that: 'A man listening to a story is in the company of the storyteller; even a man reading one shares this companionship'.

Both Berger's 'fusion' and Benjamin's 'companionship', however, are temporary. A difficulty remains – a difficulty in the form

of the question Berger himself asked of the stories in Danilo Dolci's *Sicilian Lives*: how do 'we, the relatively privileged read such a book? . . . how [do] we translate these stories into our own experience?'[16] Can Berger's book, in other words, be more than 'sensitivity training for those who keep the peasants down'?[17]

To pretend that this difficulty is not there, to claim that although the stories deal with a particular milieu they have a universal significance, is to ignore and so detract from the integrity and specificity of Berger's method. In some ways Berger's ambitions are similar to those he ascribed to François Millet who spent the last 27 years of his life 'revealing the conditions of the French peasantry' in an attempt to give 'an historic resonance to their lives'. Both Berger's historic purpose and the danger of his stories being read as lessons in 'sensitivity-training' are dealt with in the 'Historical Afterword' to *Pig Earth*. Berger insists in the 'Historical Afterword' that the temporary imaginative empathy between the reader and the peasants in the story be seen in the light of the real material relations and historical forces that are at work between them. The implications of the Afterword are summarized by Berger in an interview:

Peasants represent the majority of the world population. It is also true that peasants are disappearing. They are being eliminated. Anybody who has any experience of peasants cannot be nostalgic about that fact, because their lives over the centuries have been so incredibly burdened with the most arduous work, and nobody would really wish that to continue indefinitely. But the crucial question is, in the name of what are they being eliminated? What is actually replacing them? If one takes a close look at that, one sees that in some ways it is a progress, and in some ways it is part of a dehumanizing process as well. I don't want to talk about that for too long because it would take us too far away, but I would then come back to the question in another way. Peasant experience has continued for centuries, even until today, in many parts of the world, concerning many, many millions of people. Now is there nothing to be drawn from that experience? Is there absolutely nothing that we need to learn from it? Is there absolutely nothing that, under different circumstances, should be preserved from it?[18]

Throughout the century the credibility of successive governments in the advanced industrial societies has been based on the promise of ever-increasing consumption, output and growth. This promise seems increasingly unlikely to be fulfilled; the promised gains are largely illusory; the ecological balance now seems too frail to support industrial progress with its corollaries of massive waste, short term economic gain and long term damage to the environment. In the context of the developing movement of green socialism, of a drift away from the ideal of conquest of nature to one of reconciliation with it, the lesson of peasant experience, of intensive working of the land and the efficient use of scant resources, is obvious. It is also heartening in a less specific way. In the peasant's struggle against an often hostile environment and the abstract power of monopoly capital, Berger sees the 'positive pessimism' that he develops in his essay on Giacomo Leopardi:

> If one looks at the likely future course of world history, envisaging either the further extension and consolidation of corporate capitalism in all its brutalism, or a prolonged, uneven struggle waged against it, a struggle whose victory is not certain, the peasant experience of survival may well be better adapted to this long and harsh perspective than the continually reformed, disappointed, impatient progressive hope of an ultimate victory. (*P.E.* p.212)

Such a lesson extends well beyond sensitivity-training for the relatively privileged. For Terry Eagleton, in an oddly begrudging review of *Pig Earth*, the 'Historical Afterword' compounds the problem it seeks to address. There is, he says, 'a rift between the complex speculations of the 'Afterword' and the graphic immediacies of the stories themselves'. The disjuncture represents the inevitable limitation of the book, namely that: 'There's no way in which the Berger who writes the 'Afterword' can 'be' the Marcel of whom he writes'.[19] This is a wilfully insensitive reading of the book, ignoring as it does the extent to which the stories dramatize and contain within themselves the logic of the Afterword. 'The Value of Money', singled out by Eagleton as an exceptional story, though one still illustrative of what he considers to be the general limitation of the book, is concerned, quite literally, with dramatizing in flesh and blood the abstract power of money. These are the thoughts of Marcel who, claims Eagleton, Berger can never 'be':

On top of the hay, he again explained the machines to himself. They make sure we know the machines exist. From then onwards working without one is harder. Not having the machine makes the father look old-fashioned to the son, makes the husband look mean to his wife, makes one neighbour look poor to the next. After he has lived a while with not having the machines, they offer him a loan to buy a tractor. A good cow gives 2,500 litres of milk a year. Ten cows give 25,000 litres a year. The price he receives for all that milk during the whole year is the price of a tractor. This is why he needs a loan. When he has bought the tractor, they say: Now to use the tractor fully you need the machines to go with it, we can lend you the money to buy the machines, and you can pay us back month by month. Without these machines, you are not making proper use of your tractor! And so he buys a machine, and then another, and he falls deeper and deeper into debt. Eventually he is forced to sell out. Which is what they planned in Paris (he pronounced the name of the capital with contempt and recognition – in that order) from the very beginning! Everywhere in the world men go hungry, yet a peasant who works without a tractor is unworthy of his country's agriculture. (*P.E.* pp. 81-2)

This passage shows the intimacy of purpose that exists between Berger's method as storyteller and the lessons to be learnt from peasant experience. In other words there is an identity of purpose in Berger's formal and historic ambitions.

'More and more often', writes Benjamin, 'there is embarrassment all around when the wish to hear a story is expressed. It is as if something that seemed inalienable to us, the securest among our possessions, were taken from us: the ability to exchange experiences'. The earliest symptom of the decline of storytelling, Benjamin claims, was the rise of the novel. The fall in the value of experience, which is its sharpest symptom, became apparent in the First World War (the war which, for Berger, shattered the promise of the moment of Cubism). Peasants as a class in Western Europe face extinction. Similarly, Benjamin sees the art of storytelling 'reaching its end' and enabling us 'to see a new beauty in what is vanishing'. *Pig Earth* thus represents a dual but fully integrated attempt at a preservation of a way of life and a way of telling – a preservation which may turn out to represent progress in both political and 'formal' terms. As Benjamin writes:

every real story contains, openly or covertly, something useful. The usefulness may, in one case consist in a moral; in another, in some practical advice; in a third, in a proverb or maxim. In every case the storyteller is a man who has counsel for his readers. But if today 'having counsel' is beginning to have an old-fashioned ring, this is because the communicability of experience is decreasing. In consequence we have no counsel either for ourselves or for others. After all, counsel is less an answer to a question than a proposal concerning the continuation of a story which is just unfolding. . . Counsel woven into the fabric of real life is wisdom. The art of storytelling is reachings its end because the epic side of truth is dying out. This, however, is a process that has been going on for a long time. And nothing would be more fatuous than to want to see in it merely a 'symptom of decay', let alone a 'modern' symptom. It is, rather, only a concomitant symptom of the secular productive forces of history, a concomitant that has quite gradually removed narrative from the realm of living speech and at the same time is making it possible to see a new beauty in what is vanishing.

12. Recent Work

Philosophy is really homesickness, an urge to be at home everywhere. Where, then, are we going? Always to our home.
Novalis

Within there is a void that would be filled. So it all begins.
Ernst Bloch

'Most artists in their lifetime have only one or two underlying themes, although they may work on many subjects.'[1] As an artist develops, these themes become inextricably linked with, and frequently dominated by, a third: the artist's conception of him or herself. This typically but not exclusively romantic preoccupation manifests itself either as a brooding self-consciousness – an excessive absorption in the act of writing itself – or in a sense of urgent single-mindedness:

Each one of us comes into the world with her or his unique possibility – which is like an aim, or, if you wish, almost like a law. The job of our lives is to become – day by day, year by year, more conscious of this aim so that at last it can be realized.[2]

Berger's own current conception of himself is, as we have seen, as storyteller and witness: 'storytellers lose their identity and are open to the lives of other people. . . This is perhaps why I use the term "being a witness". One is witness of others but not of oneself.'[3] But is there not, on occasions, something so eager in Berger's witnessing as to turn it into an overly participatory activity? This is not only a problem in Berger's more recent work; on the level of style it is present in much of his 'travel' writing. In a series of unlinked vignettes, 'On The Edge of a Foreign City', the combination of random, detailed observation and recording results in a kind of precious understatement. Berger is in a café:

> There was a certain homeliness there: where we were – four
> yards away – was like an outhouse, full of the last tenants' junk.
> On the table next to ours was an open and tattered black
> umbrella. A bicycle leant against the table. On the wall behind
> were pinned some postcards and snapshots of a Mediterranean
> beach. All of them had gone potato yellow. Behind us was a
> large wooden cupboard: butterflies were pinned to the door of
> it. The wings of the butterflies were frayed and torn, so that in
> places you could see through them, as you could see through
> the umbrella.
> We ordered some red wine and got out our bread and sausage
> to eat. (*W.B.* p. 19)

To write well like this you have to *appear* to write easily. Otherwise the simplicity of the prose draws attention to itself and becomes a kind of inverted rhetoric. Compare that passage with any
one of many similar passages in Hemingway: you'll find something almost indifferent about Hemingway's prose – like a barman
who sees brawls every day – but the writing is not slack: the latent
violence of Hemingway's subjects is always simmering under the
prose which is casually alert, as if by instinct. Berger is simply too
self-conscious to write as a detached observer. One is always
aware of him looking. He is like Lawrence in his pyjamas at the
water trough on that hot, hot day, *waiting* for something interesting to happen. The felicitous quality that is essential to the random
anecdote – the discovered incident – is compromised by an over-
solicitousness towards his material, by the '*expectation* of revelation'. The effort of writing is always too obviously there. Berger is
never content to leave things as they are; he has to dignify them
with a general meaning.[4] Even where this is not explicit we are
aware of being nudged implicitly in that direction – away from
what is being depicted, towards its larger significance.

Berger's eye for visual detail is of course one of his great
strengths. Intense and memorable evocations of light and landscape are scattered throughout his writing. These verbal effects are
instantaneous and startling: 'The sky is very big, the light is
stretched across it – stretched so that it gives the impression of
having been worn thin.'[5] But the effect cannot be sustained
because of the speed with which the writing absorbs our interest –
at the *expense* of what is being depicted.

Naturally these comments are not true of all Berger's 'travel' pieces. 'In a Moscow Cemetry', for example, seems to me to be an entirely successful piece. I am trying to illustrate a *tendency* whereby, through the intensity of his concentration, the witness draws attention to himself and the quality of his evidence. This tendency is particularly marked in Berger's later work where there is a sense of an over-heavy simplicity being imposed on events in order to accentuate their profundity. It is as if, as Berger said of some paintings by Van Gogh, an 'intense sense of empathy with the subject' had meant that 'the witness had become more important than his testimony.'[6]

But if there is a hint of vanity about Berger's preoccupation with the act of witnessing then it is better seen as the kind of vanity Hazlitt noticed in Cobbett:

> His egotism is delightful, for there is no affectation in it. He does not talk of himself for lack of something to write about, but because some circumstance that has happened to himself is the best possible illustration of the subject, and he is not the man to shrink from giving the best possible illustration of the subject from a squeamish delicacy. He likes both himself and his subject too well. He does not put himself before it, and say, 'Admire me first', but places us in the same situation with himself, and makes us see all that he does.[7]

There is a strong sense in Berger's latest work that he has reached a pitch of sensitivity where everything that happens to him – going to the post office to post some beetroots, meeting a mute on the train to Amsterdam – trembles with significance. What counts, what we must consider, is the quality of response.

A sense of astonishment is usually associated with romanticism and youth. The essential romantic experience is one with which the poet cannot come to terms without diminishing it. The romantic encounter is almost always somehow *at odds with* experience. If ageing is often marked by an increasing tendency to come to terms with things, wisdom is part of this general diminution of the capacity to be astonished. Berger's astonishment confirms and is confirmed by experience. His stories, like those of the peasants in Haute Savoie, 'testify to the always slightly surprising range of the possible'.

Neruda:

How long does a man live after all?

Does he live a thousand days, or one only?
A week, or several centuries?
How long does a man spend dying?
What does it mean to say 'for ever'?
Lost in these preoccupations
I set myself to clear things up.'[8]

And Our Faces, My Heart, Brief as Photos ('not a title but a sign-ature')[9] reworks ideas contained originally in essays in *New Society* and subsequently collected in *The White Bird*. It is not a book that lends itself easily to the gallop of summary, but something must be said of the two central preoccupations. Our experience of time is seen by Berger in terms of a conflict between the lived time of the body and the culturally informed time of consciousness. Since the French Revolution, history has changed its role from guardian of the past to midwife of the future: 'it no longer speaks of the changeless but of the laws of change which spare nothing'. The change of history from condition to force has meant that our dominant sense is now of ephemerality or, in consumer terms, of obsolescence. The culture of capitalism is now 'one of unending anticipation. What-is-to-come, what-is-to-be-gained empties what is.'[10] (These and other ideas of Berger's were elaborated to form the basis of 'Time is Money', the first programme in the *About Time* TV series.) Ours has also been the century of banishment: the unparalleled movement of troops across Europe in two world wars, the fleeing of refugees, the movement of millions of voluntary migrants, homelessness. These themes, of exile and the momentum of passing time, are central to all Berger's work, but in *And Our Faces* they are developed with a calm sense of the power of their opposites: integration and permanence. Most of Berger's subjects can be seen as manifestations of, or near equivalents to, these pairings: Exile – displacement, alienation, fragmentation, migration, division of labour; integration – co-operation, solidarity, belonging, universality. Ephemerality – consumerism, glamour, fashion; permanence – endurance, the enduring power of art and love.

In *And Our Faces* the groupings are not so symmetrically arranged; these themes are woven in with myriad observations, glimpses and events as 'brief as photos'. It is a book of hints and guesses developed indirectly and obliquely (there is a possible debt to Barthes here: 'the only critic or theorist of literature and language whom I, as a writer, recognize').[11] It evokes rather than persuades, suggests rather than argues: 'like something almost being said'.* The prose has the delicate certainty of intimacy; never seeking to disguise its own tentativeness it shows the marks of and draws strength from, difficulties overcome. Poems interspersed throughout the text make a hurrying reader pause. Short sections of writing surround themselves with generous inches of white page. Spacious printing urges us to read slowly, feelingly.

The book's unifying impulses are hope and a search for home – but it is a hope and a search in the spirit of Camus's observation on Marx: 'When the predictions failed to come true, the prophecies remained the only hope'.[12]

> Eventually perhaps the promise, of which Marx was the great prophet, will be fulfilled, and then the substitute for the shelter of a home will not just be our personal names, but our collective conscious presence in history, and we will live again at the heart of the real. Despite everything, I can imagine it. (*A.O.F.* p.67)

Meanwhile Berger insists that to put into words is itself 'to find the hope that the words will be heard and the events they described judged'.

> Write anything. Truth or untruth, it is unimportant. Speak but speak with tenderness, for that is all that you can do that may help a little. Build a barricade of words, no matter what they mean. Speak so that he may be aware of your presence. Speak so that he knows that you are there not feeling his pain. Say anything, for his pain is larger than any distinction you can make between truth and untruth. Dress him with the words of your voice as others dress his wounds. (*G.* p.87)

Language, says Berger, 'is potentially the only human home, the

* The phrase is Larkin's. Oddly, he is brought to mind again by the final passage in the book with its Donne-like image of love-in-death. The image seeks to prove:

> Our almost-instinct almost true:
> What will survive of us is love. (An Arundel Tomb)

That sense of almost, disturbing the rest to which Berger's image looks forward, that sense of restless consolation seems to me central to the book's integrity and beauty.

only dwelling place that cannot be hostile to man'. In the eighteenth and nineteenth centuries prose was the principal location of this hope and home. Protests against social injustice were

> written in the belief that, given time, people would come to see reason, and that, finally, history was on the side of reason. Today this is by no means clear. The outcome is by no means guaranteed. The suffering of the present and the past is unlikely to be redeemed by an era of universal happiness. And evil is a constant ineradicable reality. . . The future cannot be trusted. The moment of truth is now. And more and more it will be poetry, rather than prose, that receives this truth. Prose is far more *trusting* than poetry; poetry speaks to the immediate wound. (*A.O.F.* p.95)

As far as Berger's actual poetry goes there is often something inert about it. As Peter Conrad put it: 'Berger's verses are highminded rather than inspired, intimidated perhaps by their veneration for poetry as an ideal'.[13] The book as a whole though comes close to the condition of poetry. 'True poetry protects its poets from their limitations: it demands integrity because its force is centripedal: it fastens all language to one heart.'[14] Its energy and truths are poetic. The book puts itself forward as an article of faith; its pace suggests the permanence to which it aspires. In places, the style has an almost biblical simplicity that is inseparable from the strong religious impulse of Berger's most recent writings. 'To imagine is to conceive of the height from which the Fall took place', he says. Throughout his recent work, he comes back again and again to evil as an 'ineradicable reality' that is 'rampant' in the world. In 'Hiroshima' he regrets that:

> the concept of evil has been abandoned. Every culture, except our own in recent times, has had such a concept . . . that its religious or philosophical bases vary is unimportant. The concept of evil implies a force or forces which have to be continually struggled against so that they do not triumph over life and destroy it. (*W.B.* p.294)

And Our Faces is a book of metaphors enacting the resolution of oppositions as simple and fundamental as this.

Within the logic of the book this is fine, but what about translating the metaphors back into reality? Is there not a danger that the metaphors have taken on a life of their own and become sundered from reality to which they refer? How useful are Berger's Manichean absolutes in the real world of partial truths and incomplete solutions? Can Berger's claims for poetry, his yearning for 'the heart of the real' be anything more than gestures?

In the first place, Berger's 'appeals' are a response to the conditions of political reality: to assert, or in his words, 'to re-insert' the reality of less tangible yearnings is not to deny the physical reality of the politics in which they are grounded. Berger's religious faith is based on an unswerving fidelity to the actual: a spiritual materialism. For Berger, the transcendental is generated by the labour of producing the world and making history. (Art, as we shall see, is the currency of this faith, the sharp meeting point of the historical and the transcendental.) His faith is sternly secular; as such it attempts a restoration of the religious instincts to the human world and human relations. In *A Question of Geography*, a play written with Nella Bielski, Dacha remembers her father:

> He saw us all and the whole history of our planet from way, way above, from where everything fitted together perfectly into circles and the circles into spirals going higher and higher. The great hymn of history! (*Granta* 13, p.79)

The danger of Marxism turning itself into theology is utopianism; in place of the consolation in the next world offered by religion it offers consolation in the future: hope for the future leads to despair of the present. Berger's faith by contrast is an affirmation of the here and now; it offers not the negation of praxis but a new condition for it. Vitally, Berger's is a pessimistic faith. It is this pessimism that enables Berger to accomodate the objections of those who, like Jeremy Seabrook and Trevor Blackwell, have an automatic aversion to a word such as evil:

> the division of the world into good and evil is no new development; and whether the good is carried out by the proletariat, or by women, or by blacks, or students, or the dispossessed of the earth, it is a way of thinking which leads to the need for faith, purity and sectarianism rather than to the awkward and partial struggles by which people remake themselves, but never totally or completely.[15]

Berger's faith is rooted in exactly these 'awkward and partial struggles'. 'The suffering of the past and present', he writes in *And*

Our Faces, 'is unlikely to be redeemed by a future era of universal happiness'. His pessimism is explained at length in a passage (probably the key passage in his later work) in his essay on Leopardi:

> Suppose we say that we are not living in a world in which it is possible to construct something approaching heaven-on-earth, but, on the contrary, are living in a world whose nature is far closer to that of hell; what difference would this make to any single one of our political or moral choices? We would be obliged to accept the same obligations and participate in the same struggle as we are already engaged in; perhaps even our sense of solidarity with the exploited and suffering would be more singleminded. All that would have changed would be the enormity of our hopes and finally the bitterness of our disappointments. My argument was, if you like, a Leopardian one, and it seems to me to be unanswerable. (*W.B.* p.273)

In this pessimistic faith the basis of hope is found in work which 'because it is productive, produces in man a productive hope'. The full significance of this passage can only be seen if we consider some of the other essays in *The White Bird* (notably 'The White Bird' itself and 'The Production of the World') which represent a link between Berger's 'spiritual materialism' and the culmination of his writing and thinking on aesthetics. It will be easiest to begin a long way back.

Ever since Marx briefly raised the problem and inadequately answered it, all Marxist-influenced works on aesthetics have come back to the so-called 'Greek' problem: how is it that works of art which are the product of 'certain forms of social relations' can exert an 'eternal charm' and constitute a source of aesthetic enjoyment for later societies with very different social relations? Marx's manuscript breaks off after the notoriously feeble suggestion that we are 'charmed' by Greek art because in it we glimpse 'the social childhood of mankind' in 'its most beautiful development'.[16]

The problem can be rewritten or examined in a number of different ways – the specificity of the aesthetic emotion, the timeless nature of (some) art – but it eventually leads to a consideration of the true nature of art. The social history of art reveals aesthetic values and the methods and discipline of art history as historically contingent but this does not invalidate the notion of the aesthetic; to demonstrate the origins of a particular judgement or process of appraisal is not to invalidate judgement or procedure – it simply reveals them for what they are. As Tony Bennet has pointed out, however, many Marxist approaches to art 'turn out to be fatally contaminated by idealist categories that they have taken on board, almost unconsciously' from bourgeois cultural theory. On the one hand, Marxist aesthetics have attempted to illuminate works of art by reference to 'the economic, political relations within which they are set'; on the other hand, they have been at pains to construct a theory of the aesthetic:

> Indeed, if there is a single dominant thread running through the history of Marxist criticism it is the attempt to reconcile these two sets of concerns: the one consistent with the historical and materialist premises of Marxism and with its political motivation, and the other inherited from bourgeois aesthetics. The crucial theoretical break lies in the recognition that, instead of 'Marxism *and* aesthetics', the real concern should be with 'Marxism *versus* aesthetics' . . . to incorporate the concerns of aesthetics into Marxist criticism is thus necessarily to import into it a set of problems which can only be conceived in idealist terms.[17]

While this is not the place to attempt a survey of the many writers who have sought to provide a better answer than Marx's to the 'Greek' problem, it will be useful to trace the way in which Berger's thought has developed in relation to the general problem of the aesthetic. Berger has never applied himself to developing a systematic theory of the aesthetic though he touches on and comes back to its central issues again and again. His career has been one of intellectual activism; he has been less concerned with discovering the essence of the aesthetic than with enlarging the possibilities and usefulness of art, less with understanding art than changing our relation to it. He has been less concerned with what art is than with what it might become. Thus, while the introduction to *Permanent Red* is entitled 'The Ideal Critic and the Fighting Critic', for Berger the ideal critic is bound also to be a fighter. Works of art are what we make of them. Hence the classic formulation in *Permanent Red*:

We can only make sense of art if we judge it by the criterion of whether or not it helps men to claim their social rights. It has nothing to do with the unchanging nature of art – if such a thing exists. (*P.R.* p.18)

His criticism throughout the 1960s continues to elaborate on this premise as an enlargement of the possibilities of art and not as a reductive pragmatism. Art is part of a developing humanism which can receive its fullest expression only under socialism. Painting is a means 'of extending and sharpening the meaning of our sense of sight', of 'developing our historical and evolutionary selfconsciousness.' We must not seek to make it a utilitarian weapon of propaganda:

The effectiveness of a work of imagination cannot be estimated quantitatively. Its performance is not isolatable or repeatable. It changes with circumstances. It creates its own situation. There is no *foreseeable* quantitative correlation between the quality of a work of imagination and its effectiveness. And this is part of its nature because it is intended to operate within a field of subjective interactions which are interminable and immeasurable. This is not to grant to art an ineffable value; it is only to emphasize that the imagination when true to its impulse, is continually and inevitably questioning the existing category of usefulness. (*L.T.* p.188)

This idea is more fully expressed in 'The Moment of Cubism', where Berger claims that 'theories about the artist's inspiration are always projections back on to the artist of the effect which his work has on us'. In the beautiful closing passage of the essay, Berger projects back into the work of art *as its essence* what in *Permanent Red* had been offered as a way of *assessing* it. The formulation is less direct and more metaphorical than in *Permanent Red*, but the urgent imperative behind 'the desirable' is still peoples' pursuit of their social rights:

The moment at which a piece of music begins provides a clue to the nature of all art. The incongruity of that moment, compared to the uncounted, unperceived silence which preceded it, is the secret of art. What is the meaning of that incongruity and the shock which accompanies it? It is to be found in the distinction between the actual and the desirable.

All art is an attempt to define and make *unnatural* this distinction.

For a long time it was thought that art was the imitation and celebration of nature. The confusion arose because the concept of nature itself was a projection of the desired. Now that we have cleansed our view of nature, we see that art is an expression of our sense of the inadequacy of the given – which we are not obliged to accept with gratitude. Art mediates between our good fortune and our disappointment. Sometimes it mounts to a pitch of horror. Sometimes it gives permanent value and meaning to the ephemeral. Sometimes it describes the desired.

Thus art, however free or anarchic its mode of expression, is always a plea for greater control and an example, within the artificial limits of a 'medium', of the advantages of such control. Theories about the artist's inspiration are all projections back on to the artist of the effect which his work has upon us. The only inspiration which exists is the intimation of our own potential. Inspiration is the mirror image of history: by means of it we can see our past, while turning our back upon it. And it is precisely this which happens at the instant when a piece of music begins. We suddenly become aware of the previous silence at the same moment as our attention is concentrated upon following sequences and resolutions which will contain the desired. (*W.B.* pp. 186-7)

In *Ways of Seeing*, Berger is more polemical, more concerned with demolishing prevalent illusions than with offering something in their stead; less attention is devoted to the 'exceptional' works than to the unimpressive average. A painting by Hals means something to us, Berger writes, 'because we still live in a society of comparable social relations and moral values'. Peter Fuller takes this remark as an indication of Berger's 'lack of a materialist theory of expression' (i.e. 'the material facts of the way in which the picture has been painted') and draws attention to the unchanging nature of man as a biological being and to the 'relative constancy' of emotions (and, thus, representations of emotions) that are closely linked to the biological: grief at death, sexual love, ageing and so on.

Similar views had, in fact, already been expressed by Berger himself in the essay 'In Defence of Art' (reprinted in *The White Bird* as 'The *Work* of Art'). Berger's essay was a response to Nicos

Hadjinicolaou's important book *Art History and Class Struggle* in which, with the aid of a prose aridly appropriate to his aims, Hadjinicolaou outlines the rigorously systematic method of art history which should replace the discipline as currently practised. For Hadjinicolaou there is no such thing as an artist's style; there is only the visual ideology – the stylistic manifestation of a general ideology – of a particular picture or group of pictures. Aesthetic effect 'is none other than the pleasure felt by the observer when he recognizes himself in a picture's visual ideology'.[18] Although expressed and developed in unfamiliar terms, Hadjinicolaou's formulation is not dissimilar to Berger's own comments on the Hals painting. But Berger is disturbed by Hadjinicolaou's idea of simple ideological mirroring and goes on to wonder what it is about certain works that enables us to 'continue to offer a mystery'. After drawing attention to the 'immense theoretical weakness' of his own earlier book, Berger goes on to try to rescue art from 'the reductionism of [a] revolutionary theory' that has nothing to say 'about the *act* of painting or the act of looking at pictures'. He does this by re-inserting 'unscientific' notions of creativity and value: 'no painting of value is about appearances: it is about a totality of which the visible is no more than a code. And in the face of such paintings the theory of visual ideology is helpless'.

Berger asserts:

When a painter is working he is aware of the means which are available to him – these include his materials, the style he inherits, the conventions he must obey, his prescribed or freely chosen subject matter – as constituting both an opportunity and a restraint. By working and using the opportunity he becomes conscious of some of its limits. These limits challenge him, either at an artisanal, a magical or an imaginative level. He pushes against one or several of them. . . Ideology partly determines the finished result, but it does not determine the energy flowing through the current. And it is with this energy that the spectator identifies. (*W.B.* p.203)

There is something defensive about the essay as a whole, a warding off that is assertive but not confident. In response to Hadjinicolaou's Althusserrian anti-humanism and cool, deliberate tone, Berger's reply seems to seek to win the day by the sheer energy of its metaphors – even if they take him to the brink of mystification.

In the more recent essay 'Painting and Time', however, Berger has achieved a sensitive evocation of how certain paintings are able to contain and transcend their own time. 'Painting and Time' is more meditation than argument. Each sentence aspires calmly to reveal itself simply and precisely, as Berger explains how paintings foresee 'the ideal moment' of their being looked at:

> Paintings are prophecies received from the past, prophecies about what the spectator is seeing in front of the painting at that moment. Some prophecies are quickly exhausted – the painting loses its address; others continue. (W.B. pp.206-7)

Paintings 'freeze' time within themselves, mediating between the tangible and the timeless, the painter and the spectator. The essay does not attempt a general theory of the aesthetic, but through intensity of concentration and observation Berger *generates* a general truth which is identical to the experience of the particular. It is an essay in the spirit of a remark of Goethe's: 'There is a delicate form of the empirical which identifies itself so intimately with its object that it thereby becomes theory'.[19] 'Painting and Time' is, finally, an essay which could not have been written by a young man: it represents the culmination of a lifelong struggle to articulate the visible.

A general sense of Berger's shifting relation to Bennet's strictures should now be becoming clear. The shifting is a result of Berger's always being situated as a participant in discussion and never as an observer, of always having to respond to the demands of the time. Although he is anxious to explain changes in artistic convention in terms of changes in the actual historical relations to which they were a response, this ambition orbits, as it were, the aesthetic essence whose constancy is actually enhanced by demonstrating how the circumstances surrounding it have changed. He strips away the mystification surrounding works of art the more clearly to reveal the kernel of 'truth', the exceptional work of art, the aesthetic essence, at its centre. The more tightly the argument is closed down the more sharply the light of the exceptional gleams.

This aesthetic essence however is not a pre-existent given which the critic simply 'finds' or describes: it is actively constructed in the process of discovery. Far from being an idealist category, the aesthetic for Berger is that part of reality in which the labour of existence, 'the production of the world', is most intensely revealed. Berger sees this most clearly in the work of Van Gogh: 'Take a chair, a bed, a pair of boots. His act of painting them was far nearer than that of any other painter to the carpenter's or the shoemaker's act of making them.'[20] While events are always to hand, the coherence of events – reality – is, says Berger, 'an imaginative construction'. Reality lies behind a screen of ideology but Van Gogh's story is of 'an endless yearning for reality':

> He saw the physical reality of labour as being, simultaneously, a necessity, an injustice and the essence of humanity to date. The artist's creative act was for him only one among many. He believed that reality could best be approached through work, precisely because reality itself was a form of production . . . his paintings imitate the active existence – the labour of being – of what they depict . . . wherever he looked he saw the labour of existence; and this labour, recognized as such, for him constituted reality. (*W.B.* pp.279-80)

That is what the aesthetic means to Berger. Art is part of the labour of producing the world. In the aesthetic we see at the highest level of intensity the process by which reality is being produced.

Berger's most recent piece on aesthetics attempts to avoid the reduction of aesthetics to the consideration of art. In 'The White Bird', he discusses the wooden doves made by the peasants of Haute Savoie and then considers the emotions aroused by nature itself. 'However it is encountered', he writes, 'beauty is always an exception, always *in despite of*.' At this point Berger's aesthetics merge into his more recent spirit of pessimism.

> The evolution of natural forms and the evolution of human perception have coincided to produce the phenomenon of a potential recognition: what *is* and what we can see (and by seeing also feel) sometimes meet at a point of affirmation. This point, this coincidence, is two-faced: what has been seen is recognized and affirmed and, at the same time, the seer is affirmed by what he sees. For a brief moment one finds oneself – without the pretention of a creator – in the position of God in the first chapter of Genesis. . . The aesthetic emotion before nature derives, I believe, from this double affirmation. . . Yet we do not live in the first chapter of Genesis . . . we live in a

world of suffering in which evil is rampant, a world whose events do not confirm our Being, a world that has to be resisted. It is in this situation that the aesthetic moment offers hope. (*W.B.* p.8)

The impulse behind 'The White Bird' is the same as that of 'The Moment of Cubism' – with three important qualifications. First, the emotion we feel before a humanly created object is felt as derivative of the emotion we feel before nature; second, the stress is on the transcendental rather than the historical face of art; and third, the 'actual' is felt to be more resistant to the claims of 'the desired': 'All the languages of art have been developed as an attempt to transform the instantaneous into the permanent. Art supposes that beauty is an exception – is not *in despite of* – but is the basis for an order. . .' (*W.B.* pp.8-9)

Art is the most precise expression's of Berger's spiritual materialism: its historical side faces towards politics and the possibility of change, its transcendental side is 'always a form of prayer' and offers secular men and women the consoling power of hope, hope which does not mask 'the agony and malaise from which it rises'.[21]

Earlier we asked if Berger's appeals and yearnings were anything more than empty gestures. It would be more accurate to see them as gestures towards an absent consolation. In the acknowledged absence of consolation, the gesture ceases to be an appeal and becomes an assertion of will. The castaway's wave to the vanishing ship becomes the first stroke towards an invisible and possibly unreachable shore. The only light to guide him is the phosphorescent trail that gleams in his wake.

13. Conclusion

A writer who does not teach other writers teaches nobody. The crucial point, therefore, is that a writer's production must have the character of a model: it must be able to instruct other writers in their production and, second, it must be able to place an improved apparatus at their disposal. This apparatus will be the better, the more consumers it brings in contact with the production process — in short, the more readers or spectators it turns into collaborators.
Walter Benjamin

It is our qualities not our defects that separate us.
John Berger

Many of Berger's essays are, as the title of one collection makes plain, about looking. They begin with Berger standing in front of a canvas or looking at a photograph struggling to articulate his reactions, 'fighting with himself', as he wrote of Watteau, 'to understand what he sees'.[1] His first strength, often remarked upon, is his ability to convey the effect of a painting in words:

> The light in a Constable masterpiece is like water dripping off the gunwale of a boat as it drives through the sea. It suggests the way the whole scene is surging through the day, dipping through sun and cloud. By comparison the light of most other landscape painters is either like a fountain, playing prettily up and down for no purpose, or like water running flatly out of a tap. (*L.T.* p.63)

When you first see a striking image, you see, as it were, for a moment, with no familiarity. This helps explain the immediacy of Berger's vision and critical method. His reactions freeze that instantaneous shock of seeing; for him the subsequent process of familiarization preserves that moment without diminishing its power, without dulling it. The 'raw' and the acquired, as it were, simultaneously coexist and define each other more sharply. Hence his precision:

> Turner is often thought of as the great painter of natural forces – water, wind and fire. But was he? When you look at *The Burning of the Houses of Parliament*, *The Destruction of Sodom*, *The Slave Ship*, *Hannibal Crossing the Alps*, you find yourself thinking that it's all the same force, which isn't a natural force at all but a philosophical one. (*L.T.* p.100)

The precision is important: he never compromises the fact of what he sees for the sake of a slick phrase or verbal ingenuity. His words struggle to match the intensity of his gaze. Most photographs show him craning forward, always trying to see more closely, more clearly:

> What does the man
> who sees
> trust to
> if not the eye? He trusts
> to knowledge
> to right appearances[2]

Berger believes that if he stares long enough and hard enough he will be able to penetrate the darkest shadows. 'In every act of looking there is an expectation of meaning.'[3] His writing is marked by an unswerving fidelity to the visible, so much so that his reactions to a painting merge into a description of the artist's method of working. He moves closer and closer to the painting but never surrenders to its mystery. He insists on his own separateness as a spectator. He is the interrogator of the canvas, never its spokesman. Just as, in discussions of old masters, the tension between shock and familiarity can be rewritten in terms of the original moment of the painting and its subsequent history, so this relationship between painting and spectator can be more generally formulated in terms of the relationship of the past to the present. This relationship is precariously balanced: tipped one way it leads to antiquarianism and nostalgia; tipped to the other it leads to a working back through the centuries to find pictorial equivalents of the dominant ideas of our own time. The temptation of this latter course is to look at the paintings of the past and single out those which most accurately prefigure our own predilections. Berger has no impulse to antiquarianism; occasionally, though, he does not anchor the paintings of the past sufficiently firmly in their own time and the weight of his urgent absorption in the present sends them tumbling too easily towards him. Such occasions are often marked by the ease with which he proves his case.

Thought for Berger is an almost physical effort ('seeing' is a metaphor for thinking), and his best essays show the signs of strain rather than ease; they are answers in the form of investigations. The essays have their origin in questions Berger has asked himself. Their starting point is his uncertainty: why did Goya paint the Maja dressed and then undressed? What is the meaning of the photo of Che Guevara's corpse? What is it that is awkward about the peasants who were photographed in their suits by August Sander? Why did the Cubist moment occur when it did? In the best essays we share the process of investigation. Sometimes this takes the form of eliminating possible explanations or using apparently unrelated facts or material to shed oblique light on the problem. Often Berger's discoveries draw him to that 'suspended' moment of simultaneous shock and familiarity. As in Freudian analysis where the 'secret' of the dream lies at that point which is most impenetrable, so in Berger's investigations problem and solution share a common location. It is like the sensation of déjà vu, where a sense of revelation or recognition is almost, but not quite, graspable. Berger succeeds in grasping and making palpable that which for most of us remains tantalisingly imminent. This is why Berger's intuitive discoveries have about them the quality of a sudden remembering. Here he comments on the lilac tree in a painting by Monet, and on the nature of Impressionism generally:

> The painted lilac tree is both more precise and more vague than any painting you have ever seen before. . . Given the precision and vagueness, you are forced to re-see the lilacs of your own experience. The precision triggers your visual memory, while the vagueness welcomes and accommodates your memory when it comes. More than that, the uncovered memory of your sense of sight is so acutely evoked, that other appropriate memories of other senses – scent, warmth, dampness, the texture of a dress, the length of an afternoon – are also extracted from the past. . . You fall through a kind of whirlpool of sense memories towards an ever-receding moment of pleasure, which

is a moment of total recognition. . . What an Impressionist painting shows is painted in such a way that you are compelled to recognize that it is no longer there. It is here and here only that Impressionism is close to photography. You cannot enter an Impressionist painting; instead it extracts your memories. (*W.B.* pp. 192-4)

Description of sensations becomes a theory of affect and then the two become almost identical. (Goethe: 'There is a delicate form of the empirical which identifies itself so intimately with its object that it thereby becomes theory.') More simply, comments on the work of art throw light on the actual, refer immediately back to the world. We learn about ourselves and each other, not simply about the painting. (This is the hallmark of the finest practical criticism i.e. criticism that can constantly surprise by the quality of its illumination – even when the observation is simple. Like Coleridge on Hamlet's madness: 'O that subtle trick to pretend the *acting* only when we are very near *being* what we act.')[4]

All critics manage a few startling insights; what Tim Clark calls 'the dreary mixture of "absurd" and "sensitive" remarks' is the chief characteristic of most criticism. Berger is distinguished not simply by the high proportion of sensitivity to absurdity in his writing but by the way the insights themselves open up a new perspective on the historical raw materials on which they depend. This is crucial to Berger's method of forensic intuition: an idea, tentatively suggested by a photograph or painting, is defined and given substance by being explored in an historical context of which it then becomes a shaping part, an 'aid to realizing how we have historically arrived at becoming ourselves'.[5] Berger is not an academic historian and his historical method is radically illuminating rather than systematic. He sifts through historical raw material to find confirming evidence for a thesis he seeks to prove. His historical generalizations are not supported by the weight of evidence that would seem necessary to a professional historian. Berger's work is investigative, exploratory and provocative rather than definitive. He is a discoverer, learning as he goes along, and his work conveys the excitement of discovery. This is rarely the case in the work of an 'expert' (there are, of course, exceptions). Like a mole, the expert burrows away and measures his progress by the amount of material he is amassing behind him: what lies ahead is that which still has to be got through – an obstacle. For Berger, what is still to be known gleams most brightly; an argument is rarely exhausted before he moves on to open up another. His is a mind constantly enriching itself. He has that instant intelligence that makes you think of the metaphysical poets – 'men who incorporated their erudition into their sensibility'[9] – and 'the direct sensuous apprehension of thought, or a recreation of thought into feeling, which is exactly what we find in Donne'.[6] (Hence he is one of the few writers who can move us not only by the quality of his feeling but by the quality of his thought.)

But it is exactly these qualities that compromise his academic standing as an 'art historian'. Tim Clark has written that the social history of art should 'not depend on intuitive analogies between form and content.'[7] Such intuitive analogies (conceits?) are common in Berger's work. Unlike Clark, Berger formulates no methodological procedure; his work is entirely lacking in the kind of procedural rigour associated with Clark or demonstrated by Frederick Antal. Clark's books on Courbet are definitive in a way that none of Berger's could be; Berger has produced nothing to rival the thoroughness of Clark's investigations. This should not bother us. His concern has been with opening up new freedoms, clearing new paths. Because he excels in exactly the areas in which most academics are weak he is made to pay a tax to their strengths. While other critics may have a higher 'academic' standing, there are few whose influence has been as considerable as Berger's and tributes to his capacity to stimulate appear in any number of art books. There is also the widespread and largely silent gratitude of those like Adam Hochschild for whom Berger was, simply, the first person to explain why so much art history was so boring or those for whom a visit to an art gallery took on a new, urgent meaning after reading him.[8]

For John Spurling, on the other hand, Berger is a 'pulpiteer' whose narrow and insistent moralizing deflect him from the art critic's true purpose.

For [Berger] the function of art criticism is to help you look at life with renewed attention, which would be admirable if his own view of life were not so extraordinarily narrow. . . But after a while the perpetual harping on the sins of others, the implicit or explicit assumption throughout [*About Looking*] that a whole mass of generalized evildoers and their dupes – capitalists, bourgeois inheritors of Western culture, professional artists, consumers, tourists, city dwellers, pet lovers, users of household gadgets, motorists – is responsible

for degrading life, makes you suddenly stand up in your pew
and ask who is talking. A socialist, yes . . . but not a very
sociable socialist. Is he any less misanthropic than Roualt, any
less preconceptual in his judgements than those he despises?
Are there any of us not in some way tarred with his brush?'

Spurling's engaging rhetoric comes equipped with its own distortions but few will fail to recognize in this sketch what they find
hardest to take in Berger. Berger's moralizing is distinctly present
but it is closely related to what is just as distinctly absent in his
books: humour. Berger himself has explained (with considerable
good humour) that most of his books get rewritten ten or fifteen
times and very few jokes can survive the constant re-telling. He
seems almost incapable of writing lightly; his best prose fits so
tightly that there is no room to laugh in it. 'This article', he writes
in 'The Eaters and the Eaten' – an essay contrasting bourgeois and
peasant eating habits – 'cannot by its nature be serious; and if it
takes itself seriously it is pretentious'.[10] The article may not want
to take itself seriously but the writing refuses to relax.

The problem of humourlessness is not just the plea of a reader
eager for a laugh: it compromises the imaginative identification
with others that Berger sets such great store by. A great area of
human experience is completely absent in Berger's writing. (Benjamin: 'Let me remark, by the way, that there is no better starting
point for thought than laughter; speaking more precisely, spasms
of the diaphragm generally offer better chances for thought than
spasms of the soul.') In *A Fortunate Man*, for example, we never
get the impression from Berger's text that the villagers are ever
even temporarily free from the symptoms of cultural deprivation.
One gets no impression (though there are Mohr's photos to prove
that it happened) that the villagers ever get a chance to enjoy a
drink and a laugh on a Saturday night. Berger's humourlessness –
or rather its corollary, the unrelieved seriousness of tone – also
inhibits his relationship with the reader. The prose is full of questions but many of them are rhetorical; he makes a point and then
goes on quickly to explain what he doesn't mean by it. In *Pig
Earth*, he speaks of the reader accompanying him on his journey
but elsewhere in his work we sometimes go along on condition
that we wear a collar and lead. 'It is true that my questions cannot
be answered satisfactorily', he writes in *A Fortunate Man*. 'But I
was asking them to try to lead you to the point of realizing that we
in our society. . .'[11]

On other occasions, the terseness of his prose lapses into an inverted rhetoric of understated grandiloquence. There is a pomposity of brevity as well as of loquacity. Full stops salute the passing of each sentence:

> Yet necessarily the language of economic theory is abstract.
> And so, if the forces which determine the migrant's life are to be
> grasped and realized as part of his personal destiny, a less
> abstract formulation is needed. Metaphor is needed. Metaphor
> is temporary. It does not replace theory. (*S.M.* p.41)

Gervais sees in this tone a failure to find a common nature between reader and writer. The tone is that of teacher to pupil and not that suggested by Wordsworth, and quoted approvingly by Gervais, of 'a man speaking to men'.[12] Commenting on material reprinted from *About Time*, one reviewer remarked that he found Berger's work ponderous and it is true that Berger's later work does not closely resemble the qualities he (Berger) admires in Leopardi: 'The irony, the lack of rhetoric, the conversational lightness, and the acute gravity without self-importance of the prose.' The simple solemnity of some of the stories in *About Time* (reprinted in *Granta*) and the unfaltering seriousness of Berger's delivery sometimes militate against their being taken as seriously as he would wish. But here we must guard against objections to a tone or manner deflecting us from the sense of what is being said. Sometimes a response articulates itself as a critical judgement almost too easily and then serves as an obstruction to further responsiveness. The attraction of such an impulse is that it allows us to condemn without calling ourselves into question – and this is its danger. If we are embarrassed by Berger's 'delivery' or 'style', which for all its 'ponderousness' is frank and direct, should we not consider the way in which we are so at home and at our ease with the flashy vacuity of much contemporary journalism?

Certainly, Berger takes himself seriously – are there any writers who don't? – but he also takes his readers seriously, hence the tensions at the heart of his style: the desire to be both guru and equal, perfectionist and democrat, to be a powerful writer motivated by a loathing of power. . . He is always aware of the demands he is making on our concentration and energy. Reading him, I am struck by the trouble he has gone to in order to make his writing accommodating and hospitable. As he has written in an as yet unpublished essay:

> Clarity, in my view, is the gift of the way space, created by words in a given text, is arranged. The task of arranging this space is not unlike that of furnishing and arranging a home. The aim is similar: to accommodate with ease what belongs there and to welcome those who enter. There are hospitable and inhospitable writings. Hospitality and clarity go together. ('Credibility', manuscript)

His language is always stripped of jargon; he struggles to express his arguments as simply as possible. He is at pains to make allowances for what different readers may know or not know, to appeal simultaneously to readerships normally thought of as distinct and separate.

To do this he has, like Raymond Williams, moved between disciplines, but his work resists categorization even more thoroughly than Williams's. While Williams's endeavours have been conducted from within the security of the academy, Berger has been isolated, paradoxically, precisely by his fight for a more immediate relationship with his public. Exactly who this public is is no less of a problem for Berger than it was for Sartre in *What is Literature?*, but we should acknowledge the persistence with which he has grappled with a situation that cannot be overcome by one person. More than anyone else, he has been awake to the fact that 'one of the vital tasks of the socialist intellectual must be the resolute popularization of complex ideas, conducted within a shared medium which forbids patronage and condescension.'[14] Berger's occasional lapses of 'tone' must be seen in the light of his sustained endeavours to forge exactly such a medium. Against the accusations of Gervais we have only to hold up *The Success and Failure of Picasso*. Consider: is there any other book which you would recommend as confidently to both the complete novice – even someone who has no interest in art – and to the expert?

Berger's official standing as a writer is uncertain; he is, in the original sense of the word, eccentric. His moment of official recognition – the 1972 Booker Prize – was soon buried by the fate of the prize money. It is too conspiratorial to suggest that this neglect is simply a defence against his political radicalism – the academy, after all, has always been rather proud of its ability to accommodate dissent. In part it is a problem of Berger's own making. He has utterly refused institutionalization, whether as a critic, essayist, novelist or whatever. His exploration of different forms and media has denied him the kind of following a writer usually gains within a distinct category of work. His has been a restless career. He masters one form only to move on to another.

Essentially the problem is that official taste is incapable of processing Berger's work. This claim can be explained historically.[15]

The idea of literature and art as synonymous with *imaginative* creation, along with the development of the aesthetic as a distinct category, is a comparatively recent phenomenon, dating back to the material and social transformations of society at the end of the eighteenth century and the beginning of the Romantic period. Before, the term 'literature' referred to any kind of valued writing: philosophy, history, fiction. The current sense of literature as both a value judgement and a description (i.e. imaginative work of a certain standard) does not mean 'that writing has to be "fine" to be literary, but that it has to be *of the kind* that is judged fine'.[16] This is why answers to the question 'which is the best novel?' are always hesitantly aware of the echoing sense of another meaning to the question: 'which is the most *representative* novel?'

Literary taste is nurtured, in general, in the English faculties of institutes of higher education. The aesthetic consensus that results is, ultimately, given the social function of these institutions, ideologically informed. This ideology is inscribed in the very process of 'instinctive' and 'unbiased' response. The literary mechanism works in such a way as to generate the standards by which its output is assessed and to 'control' output in accordance with those standards. In the workings of this tautology, the ideological consensus reproduces itself.

Berger's writing challenges this consensus and reveals its workings. His writing reverses the usual roles of production and judgement: It is not so much that his writing falls below an arbitrary consensual standard; rather, his writing tests the entire apparatus of critical appraisal and finds it wanting. I am reminded of Eagleton's astute comment on Hardy:

> It is not a question of whether Hardy wrote 'well' or 'badly'; it is rather a question of the ideological disarray that his fictions, consciously or not, are bound to produce within a criticism implacably committed to the 'literary' as yardstick of maturely civilized consciousness.[17]

Characteristically, the literary establishment does not see its confusion in these terms. The important thing is that it cannot take the measure of Berger's work. The extent of this inadequacy is indicated if we think of a few of the living writers who have been abundantly lauded. Anthony Burgess, Kingsley Amis, Stephen Spender, even Martin Amis, and even, possibly, Bernard Levin all occupy a more prominent place in English letters than Berger – not because of the greatness of their achievements but because what they produce coincides with the existing categorical prejudices that their output helps to perpetuate.

Berger is one of our greatest writers: but we make this claim not as a plea for admission, but as an appeal to alter our literary and cultural expectations as his work demands. As presently constituted, the discursive formation of English society has no place (except on the edges, where he can be conveniently labelled as 'controversial') for a writer like Berger. This is our loss. For 25 years, Berger has been the brightest figure in English intellectual life. Think of the impulse that drove Larkin and then consider the high-octane quality of Berger's intellectual and imaginative energy. By comparison most other writers seem narrow, cramped, parochial. In the work of no other writer can we find greater variety and richness; he masters the European novel with *G* and then moves on to *Pig Earth*. To get a sense of his extraordinary range consider what would be the equivalent visual range of a painter: our thoughts have to turn to Picasso. Sartre is the only possible 'literary' model.

The question of Berger's variety has to lead us beyond issues of style. More than any other writer, he has sought to question and change the role of the writer. The relation of novelist or journalist to his or her audience remains constant. Not only has Berger always sought new ways of relating to his audience, he has also tried to find ways of actually creating a 'new' audience. He has attempted again and again to challenge the traditional isolation of the writer by pioneering new collaborative ways of working – with Mike Dibb, with Alain Tanner, with Jean Mohr and, most recently, with Nella Bielski. He has also sought concrete ways of altering the relationship of writer to publisher. He was one of the founders in 1974 of the Writers and Readers Publishing Co-operative which aimed 'to encourage writers to assume greater control over the production of their own books; and teachers, booksellers and readers generally to engage in a more active relationship with publisher and writer.' In 1985, he became part of the Chatto-Tigerstripe partnership which attempted, through a loose association of writers, to protect authors against the abstract power of the capital that controls publishing houses.

Berger recognizes that it is no longer enough for the writer simply to write in isolation from larger issues of communication. He is alert to the possibilities and problems created by the communication networks of advanced societies. His work has involved all the major media: television, film, photography, theatre, exhibitions, painting, fiction, poetry, journalism, criticism, theory and direct polemical intervention. This refusal to be confined to the merely literary, combined with his understanding and exploitation of the possibilities of the modern media, is one of the reasons why Berger is not only one of our greatest but also one of our most modern artists.

The other reason has to do with politics: he is the first great English imaginative artist of the post-war era whom socialists can claim as their own. It is socialism that has 'created' him. He is living proof that the 'intrusion' of politics into art has anything but a crushing, dampening or restricting effect on imaginative work. He offers a complete refutation of the notion, common among artists, that theory or documentary are distinct from and have a stifling affect on creativity (a notion which has itself had a stifling affect on creativity). His belief in socialism animates every line of his work. Like Sartre, Berger believes that at the heart of the aesthetic imperative there is a moral imperative – and that that moral imperative is now, inextricably, a political one; that understanding is a precondition for change. For Berger, as for Sartre, the principal aim of literature in the twentieth century must be not simply to produce goodwill but to '*historicize* the reader's goodwill'.[18] For Berger this has always meant the re-integration of socialism and humanism. His work demonstrates that the values of humanism can only be achieved and understood by socialism, that only through socialism can the ideals of humanism come to historical fruition. The politicization of humanism converts appeal into choice, sympathy into action.

For Berger, the terms of that choice are felt to be so simple as rarely to require more precise formulation:

> Men go backwards or forwards
> There are two directions
> But not two sides.[19]

Constant reference to 'the spiritual decay of modern affluent society' and the 'dehumanized bourgeoisie' have an automatic appeal to many leftists, but the force of such appeals is inseparable from their vagueness when used by Berger as convenient shorthand for a general condition to which he objects. Blackwell and Seabrook's statement of the position is more considered:

> it is precisely because there actually are traces of what a more substantive liberation, and a less arbitrary discipline, might be in capitalism's versions of them, that it is so difficult to extricate these and imagine what shapes they might take, uninfluenced by the twistings and manglings required to yield to capitalism its necessary profits.[20]

When it comes to the future, Berger's proposals are, as Spurling puts it, 'oracular and vague'; so much so that by the time of *And Our Faces*, they are barely proposals at all. In the vagueness of his proposals for the future Berger is, in one respect, carrying on a long tradition of Marxist writing. In the nineteenth century, the socialist case could be argued simply by pointing to the abundant misery created by industrial capitalism without proposing anything very concrete in its stead.

In another respect, there is a deeply personal explanation: an almost visceral aversion to those in power which can possibly be traced back to his experiences at school and his early reading of the anarchist classics. This sympathy with the oppressed can be seen most obviously in *A Seventh Man* and *Pig Earth* but it is also, I think, central to his style as a writer, to his rejection of the mandarin tone of a Lukács or a Perry Anderson.

> I would like to emphasize two things that are so deeply inside me that they are hardly even at the level of informed ideas. One is a relation to what I have always felt to be the 'mystery' of art. The other is a gut solidarity with those without power, with the underprivileged. Where perhaps I am a bad Marxist is that I have an aversion to political power whatever its form. Intuitively, I am always with those who live under that power.[21]

In his writing on art, Berger has the knack of peering round the side of, getting round the obvious or orthodox explanation of a painting and into the gap that exists between the painting itself and that explanation. Throughout his work Berger insists, more gen-

erally, on finding the gap that exists between reality and an
ideological explanation of that reality – even when the ideological
explanation has his sympathy. Hence, although his faith in human
potential is expressed in terms that have their origin in Romanticism, and although he looks towards an eventual and fundamental
transformation of society, his vision is not utopian. A constant
theme in Dostoyevsky's work is the fatal consequences in politics
of a love for humanity in the abstract without a love for actual
people. The 'abstract love' leads to utopianism; a love for actual
people involves a recognition of their weakness and prevents the
transformation of utopianism into totalitarianism. In an early
essay on Léger, Berger wrote that in 'a utopia there would be no
need for tenderness, for tenderness is the result of understanding
human weakness'.[22] Expressed more formally Berger's position
closely resembles that of Italo Calvino's *Mr Palomar*:

> What the models seek to model is basically always a system of
> power; but if the efficacy of the system is measured by its
> invulnerability and capacity to last, the model becomes a kind
> of fortress whose thick walls conceal what is outside. Palomar,
> who from powers and counter-powers always expects always
> the worst, was finally convinced that what really counts is what
> happens *despite* them.[23]

Here, that sense of strain which, as we mentioned earlier, is central
to Berger's best work becomes crucial. We live in a world where
millions die from want of the basic necessities of life. And yet we
in the Northern Hemisphere are well fed, relatively affluent, free
to read books, look at paintings and ponder their meaning. Many
critics and writers tacitly forget this fundamental condition of our
existence: their world is a closed one where only art has meaning,
where references rarely extend beyond other books or works of
art. For such a procedure Berger has only loathing.

At the same time, he as vehemently refuses to succumb to a
vulgar materialism which in its assertion of the primacy of the
economic derides the claims of the spiritual and cultural. The
strains and creaks in his early work were the product of his having
to maintain this refusal in the face of the rigid base superstructure
model which was then dominant within Marxist thought. Recently, however, the model of base superstructure has been chal-
lenged, notably by Raymond Williams, as 'essentially a bourgeois
formula; more specifically, a central position of utilitarian

thought', saturated in the priorities of nineteenth-century capitalism which it sought to overthrow.[24] Williams's discovery underwrites theoretically what is present in Berger as a basic and urgent imperative. Berger's work has consistently refused to separate the aesthetic from the political reality in which art is grounded. This is the unconcealed tension at the heart of his work. His whole project has involved an attempt to reconcile the promise of perfection offered by art and the claims of the underprivileged which, if ignored, shame that art and make of it a lie.

This is why it would be inappropriate to end with a reaffirmation of Berger's stature as a writer. He is a great writer, but the quality of his work is important, finally, not for what it reveals of him but for what it enables us to glimpse of ourselves, of what we might become – and of the culture that might afford him the recognition that it is due.

Appendix 1 : An Interview with John Berger

How did your collaboration with Alain Tanner begin?

I first met Alain Tanner in the mid-fifties. I was living in London at that time, working as a journalist and an art critic, when Alain came to London to make his first film under the auspices of the British Film Institute. Alain and another Swiss director – Claude Goretta, who is now as well-known as Tanner – made *Nice Time*, a twenty-minute film about Picadilly Circus in the centre of London at night. They filmed continuously, from about 10:00 p.m. 'til about 4:00 a.m., when the last prostitutes went home. I was very impressed by the film when I saw it. Lindsay Anderson, a friend and supporter of Tanner's, suggested that I meet him, and that's how I first met Alain.

In later years, although he had no possibility of making more films, Alain used to come back to London. I remember one time he was working in the shirt department of Harrod's, one of the most fashionable department stores in London, selling shirts. In the evening he would come to our home and have supper with us, and we used to talk about poetry, because Alain is really interested in poetry, as well as films.

Some six or seven years later, when I had left London and was living for a while in Geneva, where Alain lived, we used to meet and talk. At that time he occasionally was making films for Swiss television. One of these was a thirty-minute film about the architecture of Chandigarh in India, which had been built by Le Corbusier, another Swiss. Alain asked me to write the commentary for this film, which I did. The kind of commentary I wrote, although we didn't realize it at the time, was perhaps a little prophetic of some other things we were going to do. Instead of writing a descriptive commentary about the architecture, what I used were quotations from poets and political theorists which were placed in juxtaposition – sometimes ironic, sometimes confirmative – of what was seen on the screen.

Later, Alain had the opportunity, aided by French television, to make his first feature film, *Charles: Dead or Alive*. He discussed it with me quite a lot, but I didn't actually collaborate with him on it. Since that film was relatively successful, he was able to raise more money from producers to make his second feature, *La Salamandre*. I collaborated with him on the scenario, and that's how it all began.

Can you describe your role in that continuing collaboration?

It's very difficult to answer that kind of question, because in the answers there is always a mixture of natural modesty and a kind of loyalty. When two people have collaborated on, let us say, three-and-a-half films, in addition to being very old friends, that question is a bit like asking a married couple, 'What is your role in your marriage?' It's possible to do so, perhaps after you've had a divorce, although even then it may not be the truth. The best I can do is to very briefly describe how we work. First we discuss an idea together, and then begin working on a scenario. I suppose that most of that work is mine, although what is fed into it is also Alain's; but in the writing of the scenario, in a purely physical sense, I play the major role. When it comes to turning that scenario into film, it is certainly Alain who plays the major role. I'm not usually present at the shooting, because I would have no function to serve, and, in such circumstances, the fewer people hanging around doing nothing, the better. When he arrives at the rough cut of the film, I see it, and then sometimes we discuss how to improve it – perhaps it means cutting out a sequence, or shortening a sequence, or changing the order of the sequences – and at that moment I make a small contribution.

Temperamentally – and I suppose this comes very near to that marriage question, so I hesitate really – but Alain has a very strong sense of film style, and, in cinematic terms, a strong sense of imagination. What perhaps I offer is a strong sense of form, of how all the parts must fit together and add up to a totality. I think that is a fair description of our two characters in relation to one another.

Tanner's films reflect a sense of bittersweet, disappointed promises, or, at best, very small gains in consciousness. Do you share Tanner's disillusionment with political panaceas?

Well, I think what you have described as Alain's disillusionment with current politics applies to the last film, to *Jonah*, but I don't think that particularly applies to *La Salamandre*, and certainly not to *The Middle of the World*. *Jonah* was a film about what happened to the generation of sixty-eight during the seventies, and it is not possible to take such a theme without – I would rather reject the word 'disillusionment' – a certain re-examination of hopes that perhaps, marvellous as they were, in retrospect appear too facile.

When we talked about *Jonah*, before the script was written, we described it to ourselves as a film about individual dreams of transforming the world. The image we used was that we would try to show this dream like a large colored square of silk on the ground, and then the air would come in under the silk and blow it up, so it became almost like a tent or a canopy. Then, we said, we must take that tent down, bring it back to the earth, at its four corners. In a way, that is the movement, the melody, of that film. We continually are seeing a coloured hope rise, and then pinned back onto the earth – the earth here functions as a kind of reality principle. This melody, this counterpoint of hope and realism, is what the film is about, but I don't think that quite adds up to disillusionment.

Would you describe the films you've done with Tanner as Marxist?
I think that's for the viewer to say. All I can say is that I think both Alain's and my own attitude to the world and to contemporary reality are enormously influenced by Marxism. The way that we see society, and individuals in society, is continually illuminated by the Marxist analysts of society and history. I don't think there is very much political difference between us. We might, I suppose, take a different attitude to some particular event. I haven't, for example, talked recently to Alain about Iran. Maybe we would find we are not in total agreement about an interpretation of recent events in Iran; I don't know. But I don't think there are any essential differences between us.

Tanner has described his own political views as those of an undogmatic Marxist. Does such a formula describe the predicament of the non-activist or the artist?

Marxism has contributed, and still contributes, a great deal to his vision. At the same time, he is certainly undogmatic and unsectarian in his Marxism, so I would agree with that definition of Alain as a person and as a thinker. Whether his view of the world would be different if he were an activist – yes, clearly it would be. And, if his films were primarily films which encouraged political activism, they would be different films. The films that we have made together are more reflective films.

If one thinks of films whose aim is to politically activate, although not in a crude way, one obviously thinks of Godard, especially later Godard. Alain and I share an admiration for Godard, and we follow his work with great interest. My own formulation about Godard is that he is the great film critic of our time, but, unlike most film critics, instead of writing his criticism in words, he makes films which are criticism of film. Alain, on the other hand, is essentially a storyteller – it's a different function.

Tanner's films seem very marked by a consistent sense of the absurdity of human behaviour. There's a foolishness, even a lot of clownish behaviour, which seems very important to him. Do you share this preoccupation?

In *La Salamandre*, for example, that scene in the forest when the two friends suddenly break into an absurd kind of song and dance, is a very obvious scene of the type you must be referring to. But I'm not sure that the function of that scene is simply to show the absurdity of human behaviour. It seems to me that that is actually a lyrical moment. It is a lyrical moment about hope, but also about disappointment, and I think hope and disappointment can exist together perfectly without adding up to absurdity. In fact, one of the great illusions of the left is the belief that everything can always be resolved, that one doesn't actually often have to *live* perhaps a whole lifetime with contradictions, that one has to at one level live a kind of dualism. With the left's impatience about this – from which many things spring, including sometimes absolutely disastrous things – there is a tendency to think that, when those contradictions are allowed to exist in a story, one is talking about absurdity. I don't think one is talking about absurdity, I think one is often just talking realistically and maturely about life.

This particular aspect, however, does point out one difference between Alain and me. You see, all of Alain's films, up to now, have been set in Switzerland. Alain has a particular view of Switzerland, one which I would almost define as a love/hate relationship. He is compelled, again and again, to come back to the Swiss experience. The history of Switzerland and the nature of Swiss society, seen within the confines of the Swiss borders and with an awareness of what is happening beyond them, leads to a certain sense of the absurd. Let me give just one example. It's very easy to knock Switzerland. Everybody knows all the jokes about the Swiss and their cuckoo clocks, their bankers, the gnomes of Zurich, and their quite cynical international monetary policy – no more cynical than any other capitalist country, actually. At the same time, Switzerland's army is a civilian army, in the sense that every man is conscripted and must serve in the army for one or two months every year, depending on his age, and he keeps his rifle and ammunition at home. And this works! There aren't any incidents; these arms aren't used; there are no insurrections, no protests. On one hand, that is, in a sense, an achieved ideal, because this is a civilian people's army, in which the soldiers keep their own arms, democratically, in their homes. On the other hand, given what Switzerland is – a super-consumer bourgeois capitalist society – this is also an absurdity.

Now, Alain's view in these films is, as I say, rather confined to Switzerland. My own view is not confined to that. This is not to say, necessarily, that my view is superior, but Switzerland as a country interests me less. My view is wider, not necessarily deeper, but a wider one, and this means that perhaps I have a view which is far more conscious of the tragic than of the absurd. Naturally, if I collaborate with Alain on a film, I accept his framework; what goes into the frame is different, and at least part of that is my contribution and carries with it my view of the world. But the frame, the essential frame of the location, is Alain's.

That leads to the question of why you, as an Englishman, born and bred, choose to live outside of England and the United Kingdom.

[Laughs] Well, that's a question which is very difficult to answer briefly, because it would require a large autobiographical conversation. I mean, I've lived outside of Britain now for about twenty years, and I had the idea of leaving Britain long before that, but I didn't quite see the opportunity of doing so. The very simple answer is, I feel far more at home on the continent than I do in Britain. My grandfather came from Trieste, so maybe a kind of atavism is at work here. I very much like being in Slav countries; I think I understand something about the Slav character. But the short answer is that I feel more at home on the continent, particularly in the south and east. Not for political reasons, but just temperamentally, I feel far more at home there than I have ever felt in Britain.

Another persistent feature of Tanner's films is his preoccupation with the nature of women and men's relationship to them. For example, the woman in La Salamandre *seems to represent instinctual, even nihilistic, rebellion, and the two men, both intellectuals, are enthralled by her, reduced to a kind of acquiescence. Is this view of women entirely Tanner's, or do you share something of that view?*

No, I don't think that is really my view. As for *La Salamandre,* the difference between the men and the 'salamander' didn't strike me as essentially a sexual difference. I saw it far more as a *class* difference. The 'salamander' is a working class girl, the two men are middle class intellectuals, insofar as we know about their past and their background. The story obviously would have been different, but the 'salamander' might have been a man, or, for that matter, the two journalists might have been women.

In *Middle of the World*, once again, I saw the difference between the waitress and the man who falls in love with her as a class difference. There, the difference of class, however, was less direct, because the man was the son of a peasant, and she was the daughter of a worker. The essential difference in that film, it seems to me, was the difference between an Italian culture and an Italian working class history, which applied to the woman, and a Swiss history and a Swiss character, which applied to the man. So I would refuse those stereotypes of women being nihilistic, chaotic, tempting, and men as being sort of rational and ordered. No, I reject that completely.

In Middle of the World, *it seems to me that the problem of normalization is portrayed through the sexual relationship between the immigrant waitress and the managerial type.*

Well, that film began with Alain saying to me, 'Can we make a film about an Italian waitress' – there are thousands of them working in Swiss cafes, at least in French-speaking Switzerland – 'and a Swiss man who has an affair with her?' I think he added that the Swiss man should, in some way or another, be involved (in a career sense) with Swiss politics. That was all, at the beginning. So I began thinking about this very bare skeleton of a story, simply two characters, and this led me to think about the nature of sexual passion. The first thing I wrote was not a scenario at all, but two letters, one to the actress who was going to play the woman, and one to the actor who was going to play the man. We didn't know who the performers were going to be, but I wrote a letter to each of them, not really very much about the story, but about the nature of passion, what allows a person to be capable of passion, and what prevents a certain kind of person from being capable of passion. Obviously, not incapable of infatuation, not incapable of sexuality, but, as I see it, of passion.

The story, the drama, was essentially about this. The waitress is a woman who is capable of passion, but in this case, she does not actually commit herself to this capacity. She doesn't do so, to put it very simply, because gradually she realizes the man is incapable of a similar commitment, incapable of passion. Put like that, it sounds very simple, over-theatrical. As the story unfolds, however, the man proves himself capable of a kind of madness. He sacrifices his career and marriage; he is, as they say, 'mad' about this woman, and yet he is incapable of giving himself up to the unknown, which seems to me to be the very eye and heart of passion. Passion is a surrender of the self to the unknown. Everything about that man had conditioned him to reject the unknown, to not allow even the category of the unknown to enter either his mind or heart. This wasn't so with the woman, however, and so their affair ends. So, when you ask, 'Is the film about normalization?', I don't know. I see it as a film about passion, or, in this case, about a passion, or a mutual passion, which is not born. Of course, in a certain way that does fit into various social norms, because one could obviously say that our culture as a whole – our positivistic, empirical, opportunist but highly calculating, culture – tends, in his own terms, to reject the unknown, to reject mystery. Insofar as this man is a fairly direct product of that culture, and insofar as the continuation of that culture within these rather narrow positivistic terms can be called normalization, it's a film about normalization. But first and foremost, for me at least, it is a film about passion.

Can you discuss the differences between what you imagine or visualize as a film and what Tanner actually puts on film?

La Salamandre is very close to my original conception of the film.

That is also true of *Jonah*. I think the one film which differs from how I had visualized it is *The Middle of the World*. But I really hesitate to talk about what those differences are, because I don't want to criticize that film unilaterally. Also, after talking to many people who have seen it, I think that my initial disappointment in that film was, to some degree, unfounded. In other words, I now think it is a better film than I thought it was when I first saw it. Perhaps I was disappointed simply because it did not coincide exactly with my first vision of the film. All I would add to that – because it's something Alain and I have discussed together, more or less publicly – is that the casting of the Italian waitress did not seem, to me, to be exactly right.

Has your collaboration with Tanner now ended and, if so, why?

Although at the present time I'm not working with Alain, our collaboration has not necessarily ended. I think we both conceive that we might do another film together. What is true is that I have not been involved with Alain on the last film he made, *Messidor*, or on the one he is planning to make now, in the United States or Canada. This is by mutual agreement, although I think it was actually myself who first formulated the idea that it would probably be better for us not to work together for the moment. The reason for this is as follows. Basically, we made three films together – *La Salamandre*, *The Middle of the World*, and *Jonah*. There was another film, in between, called *Return to Africa*, which I didn't collaborate on, although in actual fact I did tell Alain the story upon which it is based. It was a story that more or less happened to two friends of mine, and I told it to Alain one evening in some detail, and that was the origin of that film. So we actually made three films together, and the fourth one during that time was a kind of unrecognized or unformulated collaboration. Now, in those three films there is a kind of development. It's not easy for me to define that development in very precise terms, but I think that from each film we learned something which we tried to apply to the next, I think the development reached a peak with *Jonah*. In other words, I don't think we could make that kind of film better, and if we made another film together, there was a danger that we would merely repeat ourselves. So it was a question of beginning again from a new base, or making another journey, and at that time, after *Jonah*, we found ourselves in somewhat different positions about this.

Alain, I think, was more interested in making films of a looser structure, films which, in a certain sense, were more experimental in their narrative, whereas I, because of my experience in writing stories not for the cinema, had come to a different position. Several years previously, you see, I had written the novel, *G*, which is an experimental work in terms of its narrative. But after *G*, the next major fiction work I wrote, *Pig Earth*, was about peasants, and in writing this I found it necessary to return to a much more traditional form of narrative. Therefore, when this moment arrived after *Jonah*, my current thinking about narrative was tighter and more traditional, just the opposite of Alain's. We both recognized this, with mutual respect, and therefore decided that it wasn't possible for us to make a new beginning at that moment. That's why I'm not working with Alain right now. But we're still very good friends, and sometimes we discuss his films, but in a very different way, just as friends, rather than as active collaborators. And, certainly, the possibility of our future collaboration still remains.

Appendix 2

Berger's Essays

Berger's essays have appeared in a number of different collections. This is a list of contents of four collections, indicating which essays are duplicated:

The Moment of Cubism and Other Essays

'The Moment of Cubism' (also in *L.T.*, *W.B.*)
'The Historical Function of the Museum'
'The Changing View of Man in the Portrait' (also in *L.T.*)
'Art and Property Now'
'Image of Imperialism' (also in *L.T.* under the title '"Che" Guevara')
'Nude in a Fur Coat: Rubens'
'The Painter in his Studio: Vermeer'
'Et in Arcadia Ego: Poussin'
'The Maja Dressed and the Maja Undressed: Goya' (also in *W.B.*)
'Grunewald'
'Lowry' (also in *A.L.*)
'Toulouse-Lautrec' (also in *A.L.*)
'Giacometti' (also in *A.L.*)
'Bonnard' (also in *W.B.*)
'Hals' (also in *A.L.*)
'Rodin' (also in *A.L.*)

Selected Essays and Articles: The Look of Things

'On the Edge of a Foreign City' (also in *W.B.*)
'Through the Bars'
'The Changing View of Man in the Portrait' (also in *M.C.*)
'"Che" Guevara' (also in *M.C.* under the title 'Image of Imperialism')
'Jack Yeats' (also in *P.R.*)
'Peter Peri'
'Zadkine'
'Le Corbusier' (also in *A.L.*)
'Victor Serge'
'Alexander Herzen'
'Walter Benjamin'
'Romantic Notebooks'
'Drawings by Watteau'

'Fernand Léger'
'A Belief in Uniforms' (Lovis Corinth)
'Thicker than Water' (Corot)
'The Moment of Cubism' (also in *M.C.*, *W.B.*)
'Drawing' (also in *P.R.*)
'Painting a Landscape'
'Understanding a Photograph'
'The Political Uses of Photo-Montage'
'The Sight of a Man'
'Revolutionary Undoing'
'Past Seen from a Possible Future'
'Czechoslovakia Alone'
'The Nature of Mass Demonstrations'

About Looking

'Why Look at Animals?'
'The Suit and the Photograph'
'Photographs of Agony'
'Paul Strand'
'Uses of Photography'
'The Primitive and the Professional'
'Millet and the Peasant'
'Seker Ahmet and the Forest'
'Lowry and the Industrial North' (also in *M.C.*)
'Ralph Fasanella and the City'
'La Tour and Humanism'
'Francis Bacon and Walt Disney'
'Article of Faith'
'Between Two Colmars'
'Courbet and the Jura'
'Turner and the Barber's Shop'
'Rouault and the Suburbs of Paris'
'Magritte and the Impossible'
'Hals and Bankruptcy' (also in *M.C.*)
'Giacometti' (also in *M.C.*)
'Rodin and Sexual Domination' (also in *M.C.*)
'Romaine Lorquet'
'Field'

The White Bird

'Rembrandt Self-Portrait' (poem)
'Self-Portrait 1914-18' (poem)
'The White Bird'
'The Storyteller'
'On the Edge of a Foreign City' (also in *L.T.*)
'The Eaters and the Eaten'

'Dürer: A Portrait of the Artist'
'One Night in Strasbourg'
'On the Banks of the Sava'
'Four Postcard Poems' (poems)
'On the Bosphorous'
'Manhattan'
'Theatre of Indifference'
'The City of Sodom'
'The Deluge'
'Kerchief' (poem)
'Goya: The Maja, Dressed and Undressed' (also in *M.C.*)
'Bonnard' (also in *M.C.*)
'Modigliani's Alphabet of Love'
'The Hals Mystery'
'In a Moscow Cemetery'
'Ernst Fischer: A Philosopher and Death'
'Francois, Georges and Amelie: A Requiem in Three Parts'
'Drawn to that Moment'
'The Unsaid' (poem)
'On a Degas Bronze of a Dancer' (poem) (also in *P.R.*)
'The Moment of Cubism' (also in *M.C.*, *L.T.*)
'The Eyes of Claude Monet'
'The Work of Art'
'Painting and Time'
'The Place of Painting'
'On Visibility'
'Redder Ever Day' (poem) (also in P.R.)
'Mayakovsky: his Language and his Death' (with Anya Bostok)
'The Secretary of Death'
'The Hour of Poetry'
'The Screen and The Spike'
'Sicilian Lives'
'Leopardi'
'The Production of the World'
'Mother Tongue' (poem)
'Hiroshima'
'Of All the Colours' (poem)

Notes and References

1. The 1950s

1. Laurence Kitchin, in John Russell Taylor (ed.), *Look Back in Anger: A Collection of Critical Essays*, London: Macmillan 1968, pp.180-1.

2. Trevor Blackwell and Jeremy Seabrook, *A World Still To Win*, London: Faber 1985, p.68.

3. Robert Hewison, *In Anger*, Oxford: Oxford University Press 1981 p.25.

4. Nicos Hadjinicolaou, *Art History and Class Struggle*, London: Pluto 1978.

5. Griselda Pollock, 'Artists, mythologies and media – genius, madness and art history' in *Screen*, vol. 21, no. 3, 1980, p.57.

6. Frederick Antal, *Florentine Painting and Its Social Background*, London: Routledge & Kegan Paul 1948.

7. This discussion of the AIA draws heavily from Lynda Morris and Robert Radford's Catalogue: 'The Story of the Artists International Association', Oxford 1983. All quotations in this section are from their catalogue.

8. Lynda Morris, 'Realism: the Thirties argument' *Art Monthly*, no.35, April 1980, p.3.

9. All quotations from Anthony Blunt in this passage are from Morris (*ibid*) or George Steiner, 'The Cleric of Treason' in *A Reader*, Harmondsworth: Penguin 1984, pp.178-204.

10. *New Statesman*, 5 April 1958, p.434.

11. Cyril Connolly, *Horizon*, April 1947. Quoted in Hewison, *In Anger*, p.5.

12. Robert Hewison, *In Anger*, p.63.

13. T.E.B. Howarth, *Prospect and Reality*, London: Collins 1985, p.232.

14. Lindsay Anderson, in John Russell Taylor (ed.), *Look Back In Anger*, p.188.

15. Trevor Blackwell and Jeremy Seabrook, *A World Still to Win*, pp.92, 97.

16. John Osborne, in John Russell Taylor (ed.), *Look Back In Anger* pp.67-9.

17. 'Ways of witnessing', *Marxism Today*, December 1984, p.36.

18.   Robert Hewison, *In Anger* p.110.
19.   Clement Greenberg, *Art and Culture*, London: Thames & Hudson 1973, p.134. (From material originally published in 1954.)
20.   *New Statesman*, 14 March, 1953, p.297.
21.   *New Statesman*, 21 March 1953, pp.337-8.
22.   *New Statesman*, 4 April 1953, pp.399-400.
23.   Robert Hewison, *In Anger*, p.112.
24.   *New Statesman*, 20 December 1952, p.752.
25.   *P.R.*, p.209.
26.   Fernand Leger, quoted in Michael Armstrong, 'Permanent Red', *New Left Review* no.8. p.11.
27.   Michael Armstrong, *ibid.*
28.   *P.R.*, pp.132-3.
29.   *P.R.*, p.74.
30.   *New Statesman*, 13 August 1955.
31.   Cyril Connolly, *Horizon*, January 1950. Quoted in Robert Hewison, *In Anger*, p.5.
32.   *New Statesman*, 29 September 1956, p.372.
33.   Robert Hewison, *In Anger*, p.109.
34.   Deborah Cherry and Juliet Steyn, 'The moment of realism 1952-6' *Artscribe*, no.35, June 1982, pp.44-9. I am grateful to Susannah Harborne for pointing it out to me.
35.   David Sylvester, 'Realism old and new', *Britain Today* 1953. Quoted by Cherry and Stein, 'The moment of realism', p.46.
36.   Looking Forward Catalogue. Quoted by Cherry and Steyn, p.47.
37.   Basil Taylor, *Spectator*, 5 October 1955. Quoted by Cherry and Steyn, p.45.
38.   David Sylvester, 'Realism old and new'. Quoted by Cherry and Steyn, p.46.
39.   *P.R.*, p.198.
40.   *New Statesman*, 30 July 1955, pp.133-4.
41.   Terry Eagleton, *Marxism and Literary Criticism*, London: Methuen 1976, p.31.
42.   *New Statesman*, 31 October 1959, pp.576-8.
43.   Lynda Morris and Robert Radford, *The Story of the AIA*, p.90.
44.   Paul Hogarth, quoted by Cherry and Steyn, 'The moment of realism', p.49.
45.   Serge Guilbaud, *How New York Stole Modern Art: Abstract Expressionism, Freedom and the Cold War*, Chicago: University of Chicago Press 1983, p.3.
46.   Peter Fuller, *Beyond the Crisis in Art*, London: Writers and Readers 1980, p.76. See also: Eva Cockcroft, 'Abstract Expressionism: Weapon of the Cold War', *Artforum* 12 June 1974. pp.39-41; Max Kozloff, 'American painting during the Cold War', *Artforum* 10, May 1973, pp.42-5. Serge Guilbaud's book, although only dealing with the period up to 1951, is also very useful.

47. Harold Rosenberg, *Art on the Edge*, Chicago: University of Chicago 1976, pp.135-9.
48. The Forgotten Fifties (catalogue)
49. Ernst Fischer, *The Necessity of Art*, Harmondsworth: Penguin 1963, pp.129-31.
50. Harold Rosenberg, *Art on the Edge*, p.136.

2. Transition

1. *New Statesman*, 4 July 1953, p.15.
2. Reprinted in Lee Baxandall (ed.), *Radical Perspectives in the Arts*, Harmondsworth: Penguin 1972, pp.209-24.
3. Ernst Fischer (1938), quoted by Maynard Solomon (ed.), *Marxism and art*, Brighton: Harvester 1979, pp.270-1.
4. 'Ways of witnessing', *Marxism Today*, December 1984, p.38.
5. *New Statesman*, 8 October 1955, pp.448-50.

3. *A Painter of our Time*

1. Philip Larkin, 'Home is so sad', *The Whitsun Weddings*, London: Faber 1964, p.17.
2. *P.R.*, pp.33-4.
3. Raymond Carver, *Fires*, London: Collins 1985, p.93.
4. *New Statesman*, 29 September 1956.
5. *New Statesman*, 5 April 1958.
6. T.J. Clark, *Image of the People*, London: Thames & Hudson 1973, p.15.
7. George Steiner, *Language and Silence*, London: Faber 1967, p.359.
8. Jean-Paul Sartre, *What is Literature?* London: Methuen 1967, p.47.
9. *L.O.T.*, p.64.
10. Anthony Blunt, quoted by Lynda Morris in 'Realism: the Thirties argument', *Art Monthly* no.35, April 1980 p.7.
11. *P.R.*, p.93.
12. George Steiner, *Language and Silence*, p.364.
13. Victor Serge, *Memoirs of a Revolutionary* (1963), London: Writers and Readers, 1984, p.374.
14. Peter Fuller, 'Berger's *A Painter of our Time*' in *Art Monthly*, no.4, February 1977, pp.13-16.

4. *The Foot of Clive* and *Corker's Freedom*

1. Tevor Griffiths. Quoted in Mike Poole and John Wyver, *Powerplays*, London: B.F.I. 1984, pp.117-18.
2. *L.T.*, p.118.
3. *F.M.*, p.99.
4. David Gervais, 'A Note on John Berger', *Cambridge Quarterly*, vol. V, no.2, Autumn 1970, p.191.

5. Picasso and Cubism

1. Compare Jean-Paul Sartre: 'Marxism situates but no longer ever dis-

covers anything', *The Problem of Method*, London: Methuen 1963, p.57.
2.   ibid. p.56.
3.   *W.B.* p.182.
4.   Max Raphael, *The Demands of Art*, London: Routledge & Keagan Paul 1968.
5.   Max Raphael, *Proudhon Marx Picasso*, London: Lawrence & Wishart 1980, p.116.
6.   *ibid*, p.116.
7.   *ibid*, p.129.
8.   *ibid*, p.129.
9.   *ibid*, p.129.
10.   In James Vinson (ed.), *Contemporary Novelists*, London: St James 1972, p.116.
11.   *S.F.P.*, p.56.
12.   *ibid*, p.48.
13.   *New Statesman*
14.   Robert Hughes, *The Shock of the New*, London: BBC 1980, p.12.
15.   *ibid*, p.14.
16.   T.J. Clark, *Image of the People*, London: Thames & Hudson 1973, p.12.
17.   *ibid*, p.17.
18.   W.B., p.186.
19.   Peter Fuller, 'Understanding Picasso', *New Society*, 16 July 1981, pp.109-11.
20.   Roger D. Cranshaw, 'Notes on Cubism, War, and Labour', *Art Monthly*, no.85, April 1985, pp.3-5.

6. *A Fortunate Man*

1.   Martin Amis, *The Moronic Inferno and Other Visits to America*, London: Jonathan Cape 1986, p.39.
2.   Catherine Belsey, *Critical Practice*, London: Methuen 1980, p.93.
3.   'Ways of witnessing', *Marxism Today*, December 1984, p.38.
4.   Trevor Blackwell and Jeremy Seabrook, *A World Still To Win*, London: Faber 1985, p.148.

7. *Art and Revolution:* Neizvestny

1.   *P.R.*, p.9.
2.   *New Statesman*, 5 November 1955, pp.573-4.
3.   *A.R.*, p.136.
4.   *A.L.*, p.178.
5.   *A.R.*, p.144.
6.   Peter Sedgwick, *New Society*, 27 February 1969.
7.   David Gervais, 'A Note on John Berger', *Cambridge Quarterly* vol. V, no.2, Autumn 1970, pp.187-95. All subsequent quotes from Gervais are from the same article.
8.   Linda Nochlin, *Realism*, Harmondsworth: Penguin 1971, p.45.

9.   John Spurling, 'In the Pulpit', *New Statesman*, 31 October 1980, p.18.

10.   Quoted in Theo Richmond, 'Berger's Bet on Freedom', *Guardian*, Tuesday 5 October 1971, p.11.

11.   Anonymous review in *Times Literary Supplement*, 1 May 1969. p.456.

12.   The account of Neizvestny's life since the publication of *Art and Revolution* is based on Eric Egeland's informative but critically inadequate *Ernst Neizvestny*, New York: Mosaic Press 1985; and Harry Salisbury 'The monumental dreams of Ernst Neizvestny', *Art News* vol.78, pt.5, May 1979, pp.102-5. All quotations are from Egeland.

13.   Robert Hughes, *The Shock of the New*, London: BBC 1980, p.92.

14.   Margaret Walters, *The Nude Male: A New Perspective* (1978), Harmondsworth: Penguin 1979, p.294.

15.   Waldemar Januszcek, 'Revolutionary Deflated', *Guardian*

16.   Italo Calvino, *Mr Palomar*, London: Secker & Warburg 1985, p.111.

8. G

1.   In James Vinson (ed.) *Contemporary Novelists*, London: St. James Press 1972, p.118.

2.   David Caute, 'What we Might be and What we Are', *Times Literary Supplement*, 9 June 1972, p.645. The essay is reprinted in David Caute, *Collisions*, London: Quartet 1974, pp.135-46.

3.   Lawrence Durrell, *Quinx*, London: Faber 1985, p.32.

4.   Auberon Waugh, 'Critical Questions of the Utmost Importance', *Spectator*, 10 June 1972, pp.892-3.

5.   David Caute, *T.L.S.*, p.646.

6.   Bernard Bergonzi, *The Situation of the Novel* (Second edition), London: Macmillan 1979, p.220.

7.   'Problems of Socialist Art' in Lee Baxandall (ed.), *Radical Perspectives on the Arts*, Harmondsworth: Penguin 1972, p.217.

8.   *ibid*, p.224.

9.   Robert Rosenblum, *Cubism and Twentieth Century Art*, London: Thames & Hudson 1976, p.62.

10.   Jean Metzinger, quoted by Leo Steinberg 'What about Cubism', in Gert Schiff (ed.) *Picasso in Perspective*, New Jersey: Prentice-Hall 1976, p.64.

11.   A.N. Whitehead, quoted in Robert Hughes, *The Shock of the New*, London: BBC 1980.

12.   Shirley Toulson, in James Vinson (ed.) *Contemporary Novelists*, p.118.

13.   Fredric Jameson, *Marxism and Form*, Princeton: Princeton University Press 1971, p.19.

14.   Ray Selden, 'Commitment and Dialectic in Novels by Caute and Berger', *Forum for Modern Language Studies*, Volume XI, no.2, April

1975. (I'd already written a draft of this passage when I came across Selden's article.)

15.   Walter Benjamin, 'Theses on the Philosophy of History', *Illuminations*, London: Fontana 1973, p.257.

16.   *ibid* p.263.

17.   Susan Sontag, 'Godard', *A Susan Sontag Reader*, Harmondsworth: Penguin 1983, p.241.

18.   *ibid*, p.255.

19.   *G.* p.272.

20.   *G.* p.148.

21.   Ian Craib, 'Sociological Literature and Literary Sociology: Some Notes on G by John Berger', *Sociological Review* (University of Keele), vol.22, no.3, 1974.

22.   *G*, p.293.

23.   Author information, *Foot of Clive*, Penguin edition 1970.

24.   Søren Kierkegaard, 'The Immediate Stages of the Erotic', *Either/Or*, Vol.1, Oxford: Oxford University Press 1944, p.74.

25.   *ibid*, p.76.

26.   John Fowles, 'Notes on an Unfinished Novel', Malcolm Bradbury (ed.), *The Novel Today*, *p.*140.

27.   Quoted in Theo Richmond, 'Berger's Bet on Freedom', *Guardian*, Tuesday 5 October 1971, p.11.

28.   Quoted in an interview in *Time Out*, 30 May – 5 June 1975.

9. *Ways of Seeing*

1.   Edgar Wind, 'The Mechanization of Art', *Listener*, 15 December 1960, pp.1095-8.

2.   Robert Hughes, *The Shock of the New*, London: BBC 1980, p.383.

3.   Peter Fuller, *Seeing Berger*, London: Writers & Readers 1980, p.1.

4.   John A. Walker, *Art in the Age of Mass Media*, London: Pluto 1983, p.72.

5.   Raymond Williams, *The Long Revolution* (1961), Harmondsworth: Penguin 1965, p.39.

6.   S.F.P., p.28.

7.   *Art-Language*, vol.4, no.3, October 1978, p.26.

8.   Peter Fuller, *Seeing Berger*, p.7.

9.   *ibid*, p.8.

10.   *ibid*, p.13.

11.   *ibid*, p.13.

12.   *ibid*, p.14.

13.   Bernard Berenson, *The Italian Painters of the Renaissance* (1952), London: Phaidon (3rd edition), p.41.

14.   Anthony Barnett, 'Oil Painting and its Class', appendix in Peter Fuller, *Seeing Berger*, pp.34-7.

15.   *W.T.*, p.218.

16.   *L.S.*, p.109.

17. In the essay 'Past Seen from a Possible Future' Berger briefly addresses this problem: 'The social and economic modes of appropriation changed a great deal during the five centuries. In fifteenth-century painting the reference was often directly to what was depicted in the painting – marble floors, golden pillars, rich textiles, jewels, silverware. By the sixteenth century it was no longer assembled or hoarded riches which the painting rendered up to the spectator-owner but, thanks to the unity that chiaroscuro could give to the most dramatic actions, whole *scenes* complete with their events and protagonists. These scenes were 'ownable' to the degree that the spectator understood that wealth could produce and control action at a distance. In the eighteenth century the tradition divided into two streams. In one, simple middle-class properties were celebrated, in the other the aristocratic right to buy performances and to direct an unending theatre.' (*L.T.* p.215).

18. Kenneth Clark, *The Nude* (1956), Harmondsworth: Penguin 1960, pp. 1-3.

19. *ibid*, p.6.

20. For a vital corrective to Clark, see Margaret Walters, *The Nude Male: A New Perspective*, London: Paddington Press 1978.

21. Kenneth Clark, *The Nude*, p.116.

22. *ibid*, p.140.

23. *W.B.*, p.91.

24. Linda Nochlin, 'Eroticism and Female Imagery in the Nineteenth Century', T.B. Hess and Linda Nochlin (eds.), *Woman as Sex Object: Studies in Erotic Art* 1730-1970, p.14.

25. Lynda Nead, 'Representation, Sexuality and the Female Nude', *Art History*, vol.6, no.2, June 1983, p.230.

26. Griselda Pollock, 'Painted Ladies', *Old Mistresses*, London: Routledge & Kegan Paul 1981, p.116. Pollock's essay borrows heavily from Berger without any acknowledgement. Berger's owner-spectator is simply rephrased as possessor-viewer; his point about mirrors and vanity is rehashed and applied to Velásquez's 'Rokeby Venus'.

27. Victor Burgin, *Thinking Photography*, London: Macmillan 1982, p.9

10. *A Seventh Man* and *Another Way of Telling*

1. V. S. Naipaul, 'Tell Me Who to Kill', *In a Free State*, London: André Deutsch 1971, p.92.

2. *S.M.*, p.99.

3. *A.O.F.*, p.95.

4. 'Ways of Working', *Camerawork* 10, July 1978.

5. Jean Mohr, 'The Authentic Image' (interview), *Screen Education* no.32/3, Autumn/Winter 1979-80, p.28.

6. *A.W.O.T.*, p.134.

7. *ibid*, p.92.

8. *ibid*, p.89.

9. *ibid*, p.120.
10. 'The Authentic Image', *Screen Education*, p.29.
11. *A.W.O.T.*, p.289.
12. Jean Mohr, 'Ways of Working', *Camerawork* 10.
13. *A.W.O.T.*, p.67.
14. *A.W.O.T.*, p.37.

11. *Pig Earth*

1. 'Ways of Witnessing', *Marxism Today*, December 1984, p.38.
2. *W.B.*, p.240.
3. Walter Benjamin, 'The Storyteller', *Illuminations*, London: Fontana 1973 pp.83-109. All quotations from Benjamin in this chapter from this essay.
4. *P.E.*, p.8.
5. *ibid*, p.6.
6. *W.B.*, p.241.
7. *P.E.*, pp.60, 62, 69, 187, 136.
8. Ted Hughes, *Moortown*, London: Faber 1979, p.17.
9. *ibid*, p.27.
10. *A.L.*, pp.33-4.
11. *P.E.*, p.124.
12. 'Moment of Truth', *New Society*, 23 January 1975, p.209.
13. *ibid*.
14. Sigmund Freud, 'The Uncanny', *Art and Literature*, vol.14, Pelican Freud Library, Harmondsworth: London 1985. p.367.
15. *A.W.O.T.*, p.286.
16. *W.B.*, p.264.
17. Carrie Rickey, 'John Berger is a Big Deal', *Village Voice*, 27 August 1980, p.31.
18. 'The Authentic Image', *Screen Education*, no.32/3, Autumn/Winter 1979-80, p.26.
19. Terry Eagleton, 'A Kind of Fiction', *New Statesman*, 15 June 1979, p.876.

12. Recent Work

1. *A.R.*, p.128.
2. 'A Question of Geography' in *Granta* 13: *After the Revolution*, Cambridge 1985, p.108.
3. 'Ways of witnessing', *Marxism Today*, December 1984, p.38.
4. David Gervais, 'A Note on John Berger', *Cambridge Quarterly*, vol.V, no.2, Autumn 1970. p.192.
5. *A.R.*, p.13.
6. *A.L.*, p.101.
7. William Hazlitt. Quoted in E.P. Thompson, *The Making of the English Working Class* (1963), Harmondsworth: Penguin 1980, p.829.

8.   Pablo Neruda, 'And How Long?', *Selected Poems* (1970), Harmondsworth: Penguin 1975, p.173.

9.   Paul Gauguin on his own painting *Whence do we come? What are we? Where are we going?*

10.   *A.L.* p.77.

11.   'Working at the Edge', *New Society*, 26 February 1976, p.445.

12.   Albert Camus, *The Rebel* (1953), Harmondsworth: Penguin 1962, p.157.

13.   Peter Conrad, *Observer*, 16 December 1984.

14.   'A Poet Detached', *New Society*, 27 March 1975, p.799.

15.   Trevor Blackwell and Jeremy Seabrook, *A World Still To Win*, London: Faber 1985, p.176.

16.   Karl Marx, Introduction to *A Contribution to the Critique of Political Economy* in Maynard Solomon (ed.), *Marxism and Art*, Brighton: Harvester 1979, pp.61-2.

17.   Tony Bennett, *Formalism and Marxism*, London: Methuen 1979, pp.104-5.

18.   Nicos Hadjinicolaou, *Art History and Class Struggle*, London: Pluto 1978, p.182.

19.   Goethe, quoted by Walter Benjamin in 'A Small History of Photography', *One Way Street*, London: NLB 1979, p.252; also by Berger, *A.L.*, p.28.

20.   *W.B.*, p.280.

21.   Maynard Solomon, *Marxism and Art*, p.574.

13. Conclusion

1.   *L.T.*, p.104.

2.   Charles Tomlinson, 'A Garland for Thomas Eakins', *Selected Poems 1951-1974* Oxford: Oxford University Press 1978, p.77.

3.   *A.W.O.T.*, p.117.

4.   S. T. Coleridge, *On Shakespeare*, Harmondsworth: Penguin 1969, p.176.

5.   *M.C.*, p.40.

6.   T. S. Eliot, 'The Metaphysical Poets', *Selected Prose*, London: Faber 1975, p.63.

7.   T.J. Clark, *Image of the People*, London: Thames & Hudson 1973, p.10.

8.   Adam Hochschild, *Mother Jones*, December 1981, p.20.

9.   John Spurling, 'In the pulpit', *New Statesman*, 31 October 1980, p.18.

10.   *W.B.*, p.28.

11.   *F.M.*, p.165.

12.   David Gervais, 'A Note on John Berger', p.193.

13.   *W.B.* p.270.

14.   Terry Eagleton, *The Function of Criticism*, London: NLB 1984, p.113.

15.   For more detailed examinations see Eagleton 1983, Fischer 1963, Williams 1977, Wolff 1981.

16.   Terry Eagleton, *Literary Theory: An Introduction*, Oxford: Blackwell 1983, p.10.

17.   Terry Eagleton, *Walter Benjamin*, London: NLB 1981, p.129.

18.   Jean Paul Sartre, *What is Literature?*, London: Methuen 1967, p.204.

19.   'Do not say they died', *Labour Monthly*, August 1962, p.382.

20.   Trevor Blackwell and Jeremy Seabrook, *A World Still to Win*, London: Faber 1985, p.125.

21.   'Ways of Witnessing', *Marxism Today* 1984, p.37.

22.   *P.R.*, p.125.

23.   Italo Calvino, *Mr Palomar*, London: Secker & Warburg 1985, p.99.

24.   Raymond Williams, *Problems in Materialism and Culture*, London: NLB 1980, p.20.

Bibliography

Books by John Berger

About Looking, London: Writers & Readers 1980.

And Our Faces, My Heart, Brief as Photos, London: Writers & Readers 1984.

Another Way of Telling (with Jean Mohr), London: Writers & Readers 1982.

Art and Revolution, London: Weidenfeld & Nicolson 1969. Edition used: Writers & Readers 1980.

Corker's Freedom, London: Methuen 1964. Edition used: Writers & Readers 1979.

The Foot of Clive, London: Methuen 1962. Edition used: Writers & Readers 1979.

A Fortunate Man (with Jean Mohr), Harmondsworth: Allen Lane 1967. Edition used: Writers & Readers 1976.

G, London: Weidenfeld & Nicolson 1972. Edition used: Penguin 1973.

The Moment of Cubism and Other Essays, London: Weidenfeld & Nicolson 1969.

A Painter of our Time, London: Secker & Warburg 1958. Edition used: Writers & Readers 1976.

Permanent Red, London: Methuen 1960. Edition used: Writers & Readers 1979.

Pig Earth, London: Writers & Readers 1979.

Selected Essays and Articles: The Look of Things: Harmondsworth: Penguin 1972.

A Seventh Man (with Jean Mohr), Harmondsworth: Penguin 1975. Edition used: Writers & Readers 1982.

The Success and Failure of Picasso, Harmondsworth: Penguin 1965. Edition used: Writers & Readers 1980.

Ways of Seeing, Harmondsworth: Penguin 1972.

The White Bird, London: Chatto / Tigerstripe 1985.

Books containing uncollected pieces by Berger

'Problems of Socialist Art', Lee Baxandall (ed.) *Radical Perspectives in the Arts*, Harmondsworth: Penguin 1972, pp. 209-23.

'Boris', Bill Buford (ed.) *Granta* 9, Cambridge 1983, pp.23-51.
'Once Upon a Time', Christopher Rawlence (ed.) *About Time*, London: Cape / Channel 4 1984, pp.8-28. Reprinted under the title 'Go ask the Time' in *Granta* 15, Cambridge 1985, pp.197-212.

Film Script

Jonah Who will be 25 in the Year 2000 (with Alain Tanner), California: North Atlantic Books 1983.

Translations

Bertold Brecht, *Poems on the Theatre* (with Anya Bostok), Middlesex: Scorpion Press 1961.
Aime Césaire, *Return to my Native Land* (with Anya Bostok), Harmondsworth: Penguin 1969.
Nella Bielski, *Oranges for the Son of Alexander Levy* (with Lisa Appignanesi), London: Writers & Readers 1982.

Related Works

Milton Albrecht and others (eds.), *The Sociology of Art and Literature: a Reader*, London: Duckworth 1970.
Perry Anderson, *Considerations on Western Marxism*, London: NLB 1976.
Perry Anderson, 'The Left in the Fifties', *New Left Review*, no.29, Jan-Feb, London: 1965.
Frederick Antal, *Florentine Painting and its Social Background*, London: Routledge & Kegan Paul 1948.
Frederick Antal, *Classicism and Romanticism*, London: Routledge & Kegan Paul 1966.
Art-Language (on *Ways of Seeing*), vol.4, no.3, October 1978.
John Barrell, *The Dark Side of the Landscape*, Cambridge: Cambridge University Press 1980.
Michele Barrett and others (eds.) *Ideology and Cultural Production*, London: Croom Helm 1979.
Roland Barthes, *Camera Lucida* (1981), London: Fontana 1984.
Roland Barthes, *Image-Music-Text*, London: Fontana 1977.
Roland Barthes, *Mythologies* (1972), London: Granada 1973.
Catherine Belsey, *Critical Practice*, London: Methuen 1980.
Walter Benjamin, *Illuminations* (1970), London: Fontana 1973.
Walter Benjamin, *One-Way Street*, London: NLB 1979.
Walter Benjamin, *Understanding Brecht*, London: NLB 1973.
Tony Bennett, *Formalism and Marxism*, London: Methuen 1979.
Bernard Bergonzi, *The Situation of the Novel* (Second Edition), London: Macmillan 1979.

Trevor Blackwell and Jeremy Seabrook, *A World Still to Win*, London: Faber 1985.

Ernst Bloch and others, *Aesthetics and Politics*, London: NLB 1977.

Malcom Bradbury (ed.), *The Novel Today*, London: Fontana 1977.

Victor Burgin (ed.), *Thinking Photography*, London: Macmillan 1982.

David Caute, *Collisions*, London: Quartet 1974.

Deborah Cherry and Juliet Steyn, 'The Moment of Realism 1952-56', *Artscribe* no.35, June 1982.

Herschel B. Chipp (ed.), *Theories of Modern Art*, California: University of California Press 1968.

Kenneth Clark, *Civilization*, (1969), Harmondsworth: Penguin 1982.

Kenneth Clark, *The Nude* (1956), Harmondsworth: Penguin 1960.

T.J. Clark, *The Absolute Bourgeois*, London: Thames & Hudson 1973.

T.J. Clark, *Image of the People*, London: Thames & Hudson 1973.

Terry Eagleton, *Criticism and Ideology*, London: NLB 1976.

Terry Eagleton, *The Function of Criticism*, London: NLB 1984.

Terry Eagleton, *Literary Theory: An Introduction*, Oxford: Blackwell 1983.

Terry Eagleton, *Marxism and Literary Criticism*, London: Methuen 1976.

Terry Eagleton, *Walter Benjamin or Towards a Revolutionary Criticism*, London: NLB 1981.

Eric Egeland, *Ernst Neizvestny*, New York: Mosaic Press 1984.

Ernst Fischer, *Art Against Ideology*, Harmondsworth: Penguin 1969.

Ernst Fischer, *The Necessity of Art*, Harmondsworth: Penguin 1963.

Roger Fry, *Vision and Design* (1920), Oxford: Oxford University Press 1980.

Peter Fuller, *Aesthetics after Modernism*, London: Writers & Readers 1983.

Peter Fuller, *Art and Psychoanalysis*, London: Writers & Readers 1980.

Peter Fuller, *Beyond the Crisis in Art*, London: Writers & Readers 1980.

Peter Fuller, *Images of God*, London: Chatto/Tigerstripe 1985.

Peter Fuller, *The Naked Artist*, London: Writers & Readers 1983.

Peter Fuller, *Seeing Berger*, London: Writers & Readers 1980.

Dan Georgakas and Lenny Rubenstein (eds.), *Art Politics Cinema*, London: Pluto 1985.

David Gervais, 'A Note on John Berger', *Cambridge Quarterly* Vol.V, No.2 Autumn 1970.

Erving Goffman, *Gender Advertisements*, London: Macmillan 1979.

E. H. Gombrich, *Art and Illusion* (1960) Oxford: Phaidon 1980.

Clement Greenberg, *Art and Culture* (1961), London: Thames & Hudson 1973.

Serge Guilbaud, *How New York Stole Modern Art: Abstract Expressionism, Freedom and the Cold War*, Chicago, University of Chicago Press 1983.

Nicos Hadjinicolaou, *Art History and Class Struggle*, London: Pluto 1978.

Thomas B. Hess and Elizabeth C. Baker (eds.), *Art and Sexual Politics*, London: Collier-Macmillan 1973.

Thomas B. Hess and Linda Nochlin (eds.), *Woman as Sex Objects: Studies in Erotic Art 1750-1970*, Art News Annual, Vol. 38, New York: Newsweek Inc., 1972.

Robert Hewison, *In Anger*, Oxford: Oxford University Press 1981.

Robert Hughes, *The Shock of the New*, London: BBC 1980.

Fredric Jameson, *Marxism and Form*, Princeton: Princeton University Press 1971.

Georg Lukács, *The Historical Novel* (1962), Harmondsworth: Penguin 1981.

Georg Lukács, *The Meaning of Contemporary Realism*, London: Merlin 1963.

Herbert Marcuse, *The Aesthetic Dimension*, London: Macmillan 1979.

Arthur Marwick, *British Society Since 1945*, Harmondsworth: Penguin 1982.

Tom Maschler (ed.), *Declaration*, London: MacGibbon & Kee 1957.

Morris Merleau-Ponty, *Sense and Non-Sense*, Illinois: Northwestern University Press 1964.

Lynda Morris and Robert Radford, *The Story of the AIA*, (Catalogue): Oxford 1983.

Lynda Nead, 'Representation, Sexuality and the Female Nude', *Art History*, Vol. 6, No. 2, June 1983.

Linda Nochlin, *Realism*, Harmondsworth: Penguin 1971.

Roszica Parker and Griselda Pollock, *Old Mistresses: Women, Art and Ideology*, London: Routledge & Kegan Paul 1981.

Griselda Pollock, 'Artists, Mythologies and Media – Genius, Madness and Art History, *Screen*, Vol. 21, no. 3, 1980.

Griselda Pollock, 'What's Wrong With Images of Women?', *Screen Education* 24, 1977.

Max Raphael, *The Demands Of Art*, London: Routledge & Kegan Paul 1968.

Max Raphael, *Proudhon Marx Picasso* (1933), London: Lawrence & Wishart 1980.

Harold Rosenberg, *The Anxious Object* (1965), Chicago: University of Chicago 1982.

Harold Rosenberg, *Art on the Edge* (1975), Chicago: University of Chicago 1983.

Harold Rosenberg, *Discovering the Present*, Chicago: University of Chicago 1973.

Harold Rosenberg, *The Tradition of the New* (1959), Chicago: University of Chicago 1982.

Jean-Paul Sartre, *Between Existentialism and Marxism*, London: NLB 1974.

Jean-Paul Sartre, *The Problem of Method*, London: Methuen 1963.

Jean-Paul Sartre, *What is Literature* (1950), London: Methuen 1967.

Maynard Solomon (ed.), *Marxism and Art*, Brighton: Harvester 1979.

Susan Sontag, *On Photography*, Harmondsworth: Allen Lane 1978.

Susan Sontag, *A Susan Sontag Reader*, Harmondsworth: Penguin 1983.

Jo Spence, 'What do people do all day? Class and gender in images of women', *Screen Education* 29: 1978/9.

George Steiner, *Language and Silence*, London: Faber 1967.

George Steiner, *A Reader*, Harmondsworth: Penguin 1984.

John Russell Taylor (ed.), *Look Back in Anger: A Selection Of Critical Essays*, London: Macmillan 1968.

John A. Walker, *Art in the Age of Mass Media*, London: Pluto 1983.

Margaret Walters, *The Nude Male: A New Perspective* (1978), Harmondsworth: Penguin 1978.

Marina Warner, *Monuments and Maidens*, London: Weidenfeld & Nicholson 1985.

Raymond Williams, *Culture*, London: Fontana 1981.

Raymond Williams, *Culture and Society* 1780-1950 (1958), Harmondsworth: Penguin 1963.

Raymond Williams, *Keywords*, London: Fontana 1976.

Raymond Williams, *The Long Revolution* (1961), Harmondsworth: Penguin 1965.

Raymond Williams, *Marxism and Literature*, Oxford: Oxford University Press 1977.

Raymond Williams, *Politics and Letters*, London: NLB 1979.

Raymond Williams, *Problems in Materialism and Culture*, London: NLB 1980.

Judith Williamson, *Decoding Advertisements*, London: Marion Boyars 1978.

Colin Wilson, *The Outsider* (1956), London: Picador 1978.

Janet Wolff, *Aesthetics and the Sociology of Art*, London: George Allen & Unwin 1983.

Janet Wolff, *The Social Production of Art*, London: Macmillan 1981.

Index